RELIGIOUS EDUCATION
— in the —
PRIMARY CURRICULUM
Teaching Strategies and Practical Activities

SECOND EDITION

W. OWEN COLE

AND

JUDITH EVANS-LOWNDES

D1333570

RMEP

RELIGIOUS AND MORAL EDUCATION PRESS

Religious and Moral Education Press
An imprint of Chansitor Publications Ltd,
a wholly owned subsidiary of Hymns Ancient & Modern Ltd
St Mary's Works, St Mary's Plain
Norwich, Norfolk NR3 3BH

First published 1991

Second edition 1994

Reprinted 1996

ISBN 1-85175-039-8

Designed and illustrated by Topics Visual Information, Exeter

Typeset by Icon, Exeter

Printed in Great Britain by BPC Wheatons, Exeter
for Chansitor Publications Ltd, Norwich

PREFACE

The purpose of this book is to help primary- and middle-school teachers or students to understand and then handle with some degree of confidence a very difficult but important area of the curriculum. Under the Education Act of 1988 religious education remains compulsory though it now shares this status with many other subjects. All teachers, irrespective of their personal beliefs, are expected to teach it, and all children, whether they have a religious belief or not, are expected to study it, though of course both pupils and teachers may be excused on grounds of conscience. However, the educational challenge is that of devising a form of religious education which takes both religion and education seriously. This should mean that people of faith do not feel that their cherished beliefs are being diluted in syllabuses which reduce religion to being kind and good. Equally, it should reassure those who do not have a religious faith that they have a positive educational role to fulfil without being required to be hypocritical.

Throughout this book we are attempting to demonstrate that there is an approach to religious education which is educationally justifiable and enjoyable, which renders the support of the law unnecessary, and should make all the clauses of the 1988 Education Act redundant, including that which makes the subject compulsory. We would prefer to see RE taught for reasons of its intrinsic worth, not because the law requires it. Beliefs, and the values which are derived from them, are one of the things which make us human. They are worthy, therefore, of attention and exploration by all who believe that education has to do with human development in the fullest sense of the phrase.

In the rest of this book we hope to persuade the reader that an open but meaningful approach to religious education is possible and to suggest ways in which it can be achieved.

ACKNOWLEDGEMENTS

We would like to record our thanks to Siân Baker, Joy Barrow, Jeaneane Fowler, and Ruth Mantin, who found the time to read the original manuscript, make critical comments, suggest improvements, but above all give us encouragement. We also appreciate the help of Mary Mears in suggesting revisions to the manuscript and seeing it through to publication. The final text has benefited considerably from their advice. Its content, of course, is ultimately the responsibility of no one else but the authors.

We are also grateful to David and Gwynneth, who have sustained us by their love and encouragement.

West Sussex Institute of Higher Education
Bishop Otter College, Chichester
May 1991

CONTENTS

1   Introduction: Working with the 1988 Education Act   7

2   Classroom Changes   10

3   The Purpose of Religious Education   15

4   Commitment and Religious Education   18

5   Opportunities for Religious Education
in a Cross-curricular Setting   21

6   The Thematic Approach; the Spiral Curriculum   26

7   Religious Education and Moral Education   37

8   Teaching Christianity   40

9   The Same Multifaith Balance for All?   45

10   Stories and Scriptures   58

11   Active Learning in Religious Education   66

12   Using Children and Other Faith Members as Resources   71

13   Using Religious Artefacts   73

14   Festivals   81

15   Visits and Visitors   88

16   School Worship   91

17   Summing Up and Looking Ahead   96

     Resources   98

     Appendix   102

CHAPTER
1

INTRODUCTION:

WORKING WITH THE 1988 EDUCATION ACT

We have chosen to start by referring to the Act, so that teachers may begin their approach to religious education on a sure legal footing. Since the Act was implemented in 1989 teachers have asked anxiously:

'Can we still teach thematically?'

'Are we still allowed to do Diwali, visit a mosque, or find out about the Five K's of Sikhism?'

'Can we invite a Roman Catholic nun into school to talk about her way of life?'

In other words:

'Has the Act stopped and stifled the developments which began in the early seventies?'

The very brief answer is:

'No. The good things that you have been doing are still permissible. Keep doing them!'

What the Act Actually Says about Religious Education

1. The Act is the first to use the phrase 'religious education' to describe what we do in our classrooms. The 1944 Act called it 'religious instruction'. This change is significant. The emphasis is expected to be on education about religion, not instruction in it. This endorses the kind of RE approach which is now widely accepted by teachers.

2. The Act includes RE in the Basic Curriculum, which, with the subjects listed in the National Curriculum, is the full curriculum which all pupils must follow.

3. It permits teachers to withdraw from teaching RE and children to be withdrawn at the written request of their parents.

Regarding these three points the Act is simply reiterating the 1944 position. However, there are a number of ways in which the Act goes further than its predecessor. In doing so it recognizes developments in teaching religious education which have taken place during the last ten to twenty years.

The principal clause of the Act relating to religious education states that all new syllabuses (post 29 September 1989) must:

> **. . . reflect the fact that the religious traditions of Great Britain are in the main Christian while taking account of the teaching and practices of the other principal religions represented in Great Britain.** (Ch. 40, part I, section 8)

Although the media and teachers' conferences have tended to draw attention to the word 'Christian', the whole phrase actually requires RE to be multifaith, though not to the neglect of Christianity – which would anyway be a denial of the description 'multifaith'! So, we can still include Diwali, the Five K's of Sikhism and visit a mosque, but must ensure that baptism, or weddings, the life and teachings of Jesus, and other aspects of Christianity also have their place.

As for themes or topics, we have often heard advisers and inspectors say that the full curriculum envisaged by the Act can be covered only if themes and topics are used. A return to subjects having separate slots would be impractical. An HMI questioned on the same matter said that he had only two anxieties about the thematic approach, which we share: there was often no co-ordination and no spiral development in terms of skills, concepts, attitudes, and even content. The thematic approach also enjoys the endorsement of the National Curriculum Council:

> The National Curriculum Council recognises that in primary schools a range of work takes place which is described as 'thematic', 'topic based' or 'cross-curricular' in nature. It would be counter productive to lose existing good practice and unhelpful for the learner to devise an unnecessarily fragmented curriculum.
>
> *(A Framework for the Primary Curriculum,* section 2.12.ii, NCC, 1989)

The Act also permits an LEA, through its Standing Advisory Council on Religious Education (or SACRE, which every local authority must now have), to prescribe attainment targets, programmes of study and assessment arrangements for RE, like those to be fixed nationally for other subjects.

With all this in mind we believe that the exciting developments which have been taking place in primary education, especially in religious education, can, must, and will continue. The suggestions in this book are as relevant as they were before 1988 and even more necessary, for, whatever our personal views, the Education Reform Act makes it clear that the Government is determined that pupils shall enjoy a full curriculum of which religious education is an important part. It may require the ingenuity of teachers and advisers to determine how attainment targets can be squared with thematic teaching, but it is to be hoped that teachers will not raise up bogey men (the sexist language may be justified for once) to prevent them following their professional instincts. If they do they will spoil the enjoyment of learning for themselves and their classes.

Surrey, in its Agreed Syllabus of 1988, said that 5% contact time should be given to RE (in addition to time for school worship). Mrs Angela Rumbold, when she was Secretary of State for Education, drew attention to the powers of local SACREs to stipulate contact time for RE, as Surrey has done. The figure of 5% is what HMIs regard as the minimum if justice is to be done to the subject. *The National Curriculum and Its Assessment: Final Report* produced by Sir Ron Dearing for SCAA (January 1994) specified that RE should have the following time allocations:

- 36 hours per year at Key Stage 1,
- 45 hours per year at Key Stage 2.

Note that the Act requires religious education *and* school worship. Those schools which claim that a daily assembly fulfils the law are, in fact, breaking it.

In all its comments on the Education Reform Act, Parliament has stressed the importance of RE, and if one thing is clear it is that teachers can no longer ignore it, or teach it in a casual, unplanned and idiosyncratic way. This view is endorsed by the DES letter of 18 March 1991, an important gloss upon the Act but one which confirms its aims at the same time as amplifying them. It is printed in full as an appendix (p. 102). However, we do not like to defend our subject with any kind of special pleading. It is not our wish that schools include it in the curriculum only because they must and teachers allocate it time because they are law abiding. We believe that the realms of beliefs and values, and the spiritual development of the child, which includes the study of religion, is one about which every educated person should be informed, just as they should know about the past, the arts, and the cultures which comprise the world in which they live and which have led to it being what it is. These are the things which make us human. To neglect them is to participate in an educational process which, if not actually dehumanizing, is certainly not contributing to the personal and human development of the next generation of the planet's population. See further information regarding spiritual, moral, social and cultural education in *Framework for the Inspection of Schools* (OFSTED, 1993).

CHAPTER
2

CLASSROOM CHANGES

Education, Then and Now

An admittedly rather simple view of a primary classroom of thirty years ago compared with one now might reveal the following differences.

Then	Now
Children sitting in rows	Children sitting in groups
Desks	Tables
Teacher's deck at the front	Sometimes no teacher's desk
Blackboard behind teacher's desk	Chalkboard (if any) and teacher's desk unrelated
	Team teaching
Firmly closed doors	Open classrooms

These are not only matters of classroom arrangement, they indicate **attitudes to learning.** Let us look at some of the changes here.

Then	Now
Everyone doing the same thing	Group or individual activities
Silence	Discussing work together
No movement of children from their desks	Movement to resource areas and/or school resource centre/library

The **method of learning** has changed too.

Then	Now
Listening to teacher	Finding out for oneself
Reading a class textbook	Using a variety of books and AVA
Writing, perhaps drawing	Group plays, presentations, models, involving active learning

The **teacher's role** is not the same.

Then	Now
Authority figure at the front of the class, arbiter of what was worth knowing and what was not	Partner in a learning process
	Facilitator and resource guide encouraging children to go where their interests take them.
Transmitter of a culture	

Finally, the **learning process** used to be from the top down, determined by academic constraints, now it tends to begin with the child's experience and move gradually towards knowledge.

Then	Now
Content based	Experience based
	Skills, concepts, attitudes, as well as knowledge and content
Separate subjects	Thematic linking of subjects

Before reading further you might like to consider the comparisons. Have there been losses as well as gains? Where do you stand, wholly on one side or partly on both? (The purpose of this book is to help you work out your own approaches to teaching, not to brainwash you into accepting ours.)

Now, of course, this outline is a generalization. Some readers will already be recalling the active learning they enjoyed in their primary schools. Some may be able to name a school where children still sit in rows and are passive learners. This is seldom true of mathematics or science, though. It must be some considerable time since the teacher worked a few examples on the board and then set the whole class ten sums to practise on for themselves, or told them *about* pond life but never allowed them to visit a pond or experience pond-dipping. However, in religious education and probably history one is still likely to find the tradition of bottoms on seats, everyone listening to a story, very much alive.

Why this difference between, say, RE and mathematics? Here are several reasons. You may like to evaluate them and add others of your own.

- Children like stories and teachers love telling them. (There aren't many good stories in maths, or if there are someone is keeping quiet about them.)
- Stories are an important part of our heritage. Children should know them.
- It is the way we were taught history and RE and *we* enjoyed the approach.
- It is the way we were taught history and RE and we tend to use the same methods, especially if they seemed to succeed with us.
- Maths has had to change because it was realized that passive methods of learning were unsuccessful. Even the minority who coped with the rote-learning approach tended not to become numerate in the sense of understanding what they were doing. They simply memorized information and were able to recapitulate the teacher's methodology. Change was imposed as a result of pressure from employers and researchers in mathematics education as well as the professional common sense of teachers.

● No one has compelled teachers to change their approach to humanities teaching. With so many areas of the curriculum to cover, not to mention assessment, it is only natural that they keep to well-tried and apparently successful ways, though many teachers now doubt the efficacy of this approach to the humanities and are finding active learning methods more satisfactory and more enjoyable for themselves and the children.

Although we value stories, as should be clear by the time you reach the end of this book, we cannot share the view that the story-dominated approach to religious education is successful. You might like to test it for yourself.

Take a story which you normally tell, see how many children can recall it accurately, and then question them about it to discover how many of them have understood it.

Often we are satisfied if the ablest twenty per cent, children like ourselves, provide intelligent answers which demonstrate their grasp of what they have been told. Perhaps we should be more concerned about the rest: those like our friends who found school boring and left as soon as they could, or anyway rejected religion; those like other children we may remember who were failures, often because the system was geared to making them fail by the conditions it imposed for achieving success – the ability to read, remember, and regurgitate answers. They preferred to do things.

Many schoolchild howlers are really the product of pupils not understanding ideas which lie outside their experience. Recently, a girl told her mother how the wise men travelled to see Jesus: they came by boat. 'They were shipped in,' she said. 'Worshipped him' was beyond her comprehension, so she coped as best she could. The old chestnut 'Harold be thy name' is the product of similar effort, not stupidity. How many of us, even now, would like to explain 'hallowed', 'holy' or 'worship' to our adult peers?

At an even simpler level, if you ask a three-year-old to recite 'I'm a little teapot, short and stout . . .', you might actually catch them saying 'I'm a little teapot, short and spout; here's my handle, here's my spout', because 'stout' is not a very common word nowadays, even if the physical condition is familiar enough! It may not matter if they get a nursery rhyme wrong, but stories from the Bible or other scriptures belong to a far more serious category. We shouldn't be inviting children to make nonsense of them.

Deprived of the use of stories, just for the time being, what have we left? There is the child's experience and tangible objects to begin with.

Beginning with Experience – Implicit RE

Here we are talking not about religious experience but about feelings and events which are part of the child's life. S/he knows the excitement of preparing for a holiday, or a party, or the arrival of grandparents, or perhaps a new baby. These are the kinds of experiences that we might begin with before introducing explicitly religious material or concepts. Often we call this the implicit approach. Opposite are two examples from the classroom.

The relating of facts to experience to give them meaning is not confined to young children of course. Literature, the arts in general, history and religion link the two together. When we say that something is irrelevant we mean that it doesn't fit in with our experience of life or help make sense of it.

Techniques such as role-play, discussion, art and craft which are used extensively to enhance other curriculum areas can be employed in religious education to make it more

Two Examples of Implicit RE

The children sat on the carpet around their teacher. She told them that they were going on a journey. What would they need? Some replies were direct and unquestioning: 'Food', 'Clothes', 'A case to put things in', 'Money'. Others took the form of questions: 'Where are we going?', 'Will it be hot there?', 'How long are we going for?', 'Why are we going?' Gradually the class began to realize the need for planning and preparation, for suitable or special clothes, and that the journey might be undertaken for lots of different reasons, some more important than others.

The teacher then came on to the Hajj, the pilgrimage to Makkah that all Muslims should make at least once. She was able to show the children the special clothes that Muslims wear and pictures of the places they would visit, and explain something of the importance that the Hajj has for Muslims. She felt, however, that this explicit material made sense to her class because they had begun with experiences in their own lives which are implicit in the Muslim pilgrimage – such things as preparation, excitement, and doing something important, as well as just going on a journey.

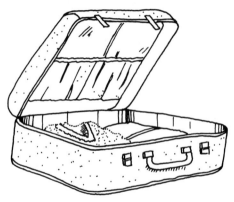

Another starting-point was a simple party. After morning break the class came in to find bottles of squash and plastic beakers, and some biscuits on plates waiting for them. 'Let's have a party,' said the teacher. Before long Alice, who had been miserable earlier on, was smiling. Peter and James, who hadn't been speaking to one another, were laughing together. Even the shy children were becoming noisy! Amid the eating the inquisitive members of the class started to ask why they were having a party:

'Sir's birthday', 'He's getting married', 'Winning the pools'

were among the suggested reasons.

Out of the situation it was possible to explore how we feel when we have parties and why we have them. From this implicit beginning it was then easy to proceed to religious celebrations and festivals, homing in on Easter and the Hindu festival of Holi, looking at the things that Christians and Hindus do, and the stories they tell, and arriving at some understanding of what these festivals mean to believers.

interesting, intelligible and enjoyable. It should be fun as much as any other activity that children do and should be the equal of any in terms of being stimulating.

You might like to ask yourself where you stand along the following lines:

Teacher
Informer ——————————————————————— **Facilitator**

Approach
Passive learning ——————————————————— **Active learning**

Most teachers would probably place themselves somewhere along each line rather than at one end but probably moving towards the right.

Active learning in religious education is discussed in more detail in Chapter 11, and ideas and guidelines for particular active learning techniques are given in Chapters 12–15.

CHAPTER
3
THE PURPOSE OF RELIGIOUS EDUCATION

The Teacher

The key figure in the educational process is the teacher, especially in those curriculum areas which society does not seem to value. This is particularly true of history, religious education, geography, music and art. The teacher's attitude rubs off. How often have we heard children say:

'I didn't used to like school, but now we've got Ms ****, she's super.'

or

'I liked maths but this year we've got Mr **** '?

Education is not neutral. We may try to avoid influencing children by teaching only facts but even our choice of which facts to teach conveys a message. It may be of the squalor of life in Victorian England. It may be of the greatness of our Victorian ancestors as they completed the annexation of India for the Empire. Perhaps it is the way that we gave refuge to Jews in the twentieth century or the story of their expulsion in 1290. Or we may cover both. Geography can focus on Britain or can inform pupils that the rest of the world is also fascinating and worth knowing about. The literature we use is capable of telling us that 'a single shelf of a good European library is worth the whole native literature of India and Arabia', to quote Thomas Babington Macaulay, just by never mentioning anything that is not European. When the selection is confined to Britain it confirms us in our insular prejudices.

Omission is also a form of selection. No drama, little art, but plenty of maths is as much a statement of what matters as actually telling children that music or poetry is a waste of time. This is why it is essential to provide a balanced curriculum in which all subjects are valued. One area or another may not be of great interest to us, or be our strength, but teachers know that education should not be about teacher self-indulgence of likes and avoidance of dislikes, and we cannot assume, as we dodge another music lesson, that all will come right in the end because 'Mr Jones will have them next year, he likes singing'.

At this point you might work out how much time you have given to things that are recognizably music, art, drama, or religious education in the last fortnight.

Religious education is also affected by the teacher's beliefs. The religious believer is likely to be a Christian, who may wish to persuade pupils of the truth of Christianity. Other teachers are likely to have a British Christian heritage but no personal faith. They may feel hypocritical communicating beliefs they do not hold. There are also teachers from religious minorities, far too few of them. They may likewise be embarrassed at being required to teach about a religion which is not theirs and which may actually seem to deny the truths which they treasure.

When the purpose of RE was to nurture children in the Christian faith it was impossible for anyone to teach RE who was not a Christian. If, however, RE can have other aims, we feel convinced that all teachers will be able to teach it.

Here are some aims. Which of them can all teachers be expected to accept?

We speak of religious education, but we mean Christian education. The aim of Christian education in its full and proper sense is quite simply to confront our children with Jesus Christ. (Birmingham Agreed Syllabus, 1962)

The aim [of RE] is to help young people to achieve a knowledge and understanding of religious insights, beliefs and practices, so that they are able to continue in or come to, their own beliefs and respect the right of other people to hold beliefs different from their own.

While it is taken for granted that Christianity features clearly, the syllabus also provides for teaching about other important faiths which are held in contemporary British society. It is no part of the responsibility of the county school to promote any particular religious standpoint. (ILEA Agreed Syllabus, 1984)

The principal aim of RE in schools within the public sector is to enable pupils to understand the nature of religious beliefs and practices, and the importance and influence of these in the lives of believers. (West Sussex Agreed Syllabus, 1983)

EXPLORING MEANING. Developing an awareness of the spiritual dimension of life. (Hampshire Agreed Syllabus, 1992)

Before reading further it might be helpful to reflect upon these three aims, which represent the main attitudes towards RE.

- **You might be able to accept one of them and make it your own.**
- **You might create your own aim drawing on ideas from those quoted.**

We suggest that you write down the aim and consider how what you actually teach matches it.

- **If you are using the book for staff discussion, what aim can you all agree on?**

The first aim is one which only Christian teachers could accept, and then only if they considered it their duty to evangelize in school or nurture pupils in the Christian faith. It is one which many teachers still think, quite incorrectly, that the law requires. Not surprisingly, therefore, they try to avoid teaching RE. This may explain why recently, out of a group of thirty-five students who had been working in Hampshire and West Sussex primary schools, only eight had experienced anything which they could recognize as being religious education. Many Christian teachers do not believe that schools should be used for the purpose of evangelism or nurture. These they regard as the privilege and responsibility of parents and the faith communities.

The ILEA aim implies that young people have a faith or should come to hold one. Even though that faith may not be religious should schools be striving to persuade pupils to make some kind of commitment? This is an issue for all teachers and staffrooms to face. It isn't confined to RE though it is usually shrugged off onto it. We suggested earlier that all education is affective, though the agenda may sometimes be hidden and perhaps unintentional. How affective should it be? Most teachers would agree that it should be positive in affirming equality of sex and race as well as promoting social equality. If it is proper to have these aims why should education not endorse other beliefs and values, many of them based on religion, and commend them to children? Is it simply because most adults are unsure about these things themselves and so are uneasy about hypocritically presenting them to those they teach?

Here you might like to pause to think or discuss and then write down your own list of the values which you believe you should be inculcating.

The West Sussex aim confines itself to 'religious beliefs and practices' but also restricts itself to understanding. It can be adopted by any teacher regardless of her or his personal beliefs so long as it is accepted that religion is an area of life which everyone should know about and that evangelism is inappropriate in the classroom. Here we would remind teachers of the DES letter of 18 March 1991, which states that an Agreed Syllabus should:

> not be designed to convert pupils, or urge a particular religion or religious belief on pupils

(see p. 102, where the letter is printed in full). Such religious education is fair in the demands it makes upon the teacher and pupil, respecting the personal positions of both. This approach has many advocates. It asks that RE is taught in such a way that pupils understand what it means to take religion seriously, to be committed, but it rejects attempts to influence them towards, or against, such commitment. Its proponents would argue that in teaching RE they have no more responsibility for influencing children, and no less, of course, than in any other subject. Their purpose is precisely the same as that of the scientist, mathematician or historian. By taking this stand the RE teacher is asking the school as a whole, and society to decide what its values are. (Further discussion of this issue may be found in the next chapter.)

The argument that Britain is a Christian country has often allowed, or compelled, everyone else to opt out of the values debate. They have been made to feel that their views and insights are irrelevant or unwelcome. Religious education must not be permitted to convey the same message in our schools. They belong to society as a whole and should not be places where any group is privileged or feels marginalized or even excluded.

CHAPTER
4

COMMITMENT AND RELIGIOUS EDUCATION

Much has been written about this matter, often from the standpoint of the teacher. This is important of course, but let us remember as well the child, the subject and the purpose of education in a democracy such as Britain. The teacher is, or should be, someone who can take care of her/himself. S/he enjoys an extremely privileged position as someone responsible for forming the attitudes of children as well as helping develop their concepts and skills. Governments may not rate teachers highly but society should. In this context we might ask what should be a teacher's first commitment?

You might like to reflect on this from your own perspective before reading further.

A Muslim or Christian, or a Humanist could reply that it is to their faith. Their reply would be quite proper. Teaching would be a vocation for them, the consequence of their belief. However, how do we expect faith to cash out in practice in the classroom? Should it appear as evangelism or as heightened professionalism – and what does that glib phrase mean? We leave you to consider what difference you would expect to find in a teacher motivated by a particular religious belief or life stance as opposed to one who has decided to enter the profession for the same reasons that one might become a banker, accountant, or take up a career in management. We can already hear the cries of complaint from those who are Christian bankers or career teachers!

When it comes to teaching RE who should do it better, the believer or the non-believer? Views on this vary considerably on lines such as the following:

- Only the believer can put across the feel of a religion.
- A believer is bound to be insensitive to the doubts and views of those who don't share his/her beliefs.
- Believers stand so close to their beliefs that they cannot be objective.
- You have to experience something (like worship) to teach about it.

Each of these arguments has some weight. We have known people who would not accept any label who are excellent teachers of the kind of RE described in this book. We have also come across Christians, Humanists and others who were unable to cope with its demands. Whatever religion one is teaching it is important that sooner or later the children should meet adherents or, if that is not possible, read material written by them. The children should also watch videos or attend acts of worship of the faiths being studied. (School worship is no substitute for this. Most participants do not stand within the faith, or even on the threshold! They are streets away!)

Successful RE teaching within the aims put forward in this book is primarily a professional exercise. The teacher has to suspend judgement and his/her own beliefs in order to present sympathetically and accurately the views being examined. Here the situation is not unique. The Jew who lost relatives in the Holocaust has probably a much more difficult problem to cope with if s/he is to teach the history of the Third Reich successfully. Some Jews might not be able to do that, some ex-prisoners of the Japanese might not be able to examine the Second World War in the Pacific. Some Muslims might not be able to help children understand Christian beliefs which are at variance with the Qur'an. Some Christians may have the same kind of difficulty in teaching the Muslim view of Jesus.

At the end of the day it is preferable that these people are honest rather than hypocritical, and do not teach things with which they cannot cope even after having made a sincere effort, especially to younger children who may not be able to detect their position. However, anyone who falls into this category should ask themself, 'How can we expect children to do what we cannot manage?' Is it reasonable to ask a Muslim child, for example, to try to understand what Jesus means to Christians if a Christian teacher says s/he cannot teach the Muslim view of him? The logical consequence of this position is the end of education and an admission that we can only understand ourselves!

Here we come to the point of realizing that the child has a background of belief as well as the teacher. Tenderness of conscience is not something adults should talk about to the neglect of the vulnerable susceptibilities of the children for whom they are responsible.

Imagine you are a Muslim child and your teacher tells you, 'Now you are living here you must learn about our religion,' and in every way informs you that what you possess has no worth: your language, the foods you eat, the colour of your skin, and your parental faith. Even your name is a problem. Even if one wished to convert the child to Christianity it would be bad tactically to begin by (implicitly or explicitly) devaluing these things, which are all s/he has got, and a poor witness to Jesus, who respected men and women for what they were. It is not religions but racism and certain political ideologies of an extreme left- or right-wing nature which devalue the individual in this way.

Finally, then, classroom evangelism in our maintained schools would seem to be untrue to the precepts of the great religions and an intrusion upon the basic human right to freedom of religion. Many would prefer RE not to exist than be used for sectarian purposes, and those who hold such a view include believers, a lot of them Christians, but others Baha'is, Buddhists, Hindus, Humanists, Jews or Sikhs.

Abandoning RE would leave children ignorant and a prey to those unscrupulous groups in all societies which wish to manipulate them for narrow religious or racist purposes. Fortunately, this is not the only alternative to evangelism. The approach set out in this book is a form of RE which examines beliefs and values in an open way which is respectful to the traditions being studied and to the home faith, if they have one, which children bring to school. It is commitment to this kind of RE that teachers should be seeking to promote, in the context of an education which has similar aims. It must, of necessity, be critical, in the best sense of the word, and this may be alarming to some believers in all the major faiths as well as to those politicians who see education more as an agent for nurturing children into a culture and predetermined set of values rather than a process which is constantly challenging accepted norms and nostrums. Here religious education finds itself caught up in a greater debate to which it has much to offer and from which it can disengage only if it is prepared to lose its vitality and worth.

Sometimes we are accused of relativism, of suggesting through our religious-studies approach to religious education that all religions are relatively true but none is *the* true religion. This is to misunderstand our aim, which is for children to understand religions in the fullest sense of the word. This includes helping children to appreciate what it means to take a religion seriously; how a Christian's or Buddhist's faith affects her/his whole outlook on life. Pupils should also examine at an appropriate stage, in the secondary school, how believers who claim that their religion is true respond to the other faiths, whose existence they have now to acknowledge even though believers often ignored them in the past. This can then be done in the only proper context, one of understanding and knowing about a variety of life stances in an open way without assertion by school or teacher of the supremacy of any, and from a position of respect for each. The primary school has played its part by providing some knowledge and understanding, but even more important, respect for the worth of each child including the beliefs, if any, which s/he brings from home to the school.

CHAPTER
5

OPPORTUNITIES FOR RELIGIOUS EDUCATION IN A CROSS-CURRICULAR SETTING

Most teachers in the primary classroom feel that particular subject disciplines can be approached through a general theme or topic. Geography and history, for example, tend to be tackled by exploring themes such as 'The Environment', 'Farms and Farming' or 'Water', rather than as separate subjects, and National Curriculum documents endorse this cross-curricular approach.

For many years, however, religious education was viewed as somehow different and either taught separately (and called 'Scripture' in our youth) or omitted totally from the curriculum by those who felt confused, unqualified or embarrassed. The legacy is still evident in some primary classrooms, and although teachers acknowledge the importance of RE, they find it difficult to place in today's curriculum and feel concern that RE can become lost in a cross-curricular soup. Religious education can be fully integrated or taught separately. A closer look at what it consists of should help teachers to locate RE and maintain its identity within the curriculum.

Most Agreed Syllabuses for RE focus on four main areas which together should provide a balanced RE diet throughout a child's schooling. Check these areas with your own local Agreed Syllabus for RE if possible.

1. Awareness of Self

Young children are naturally egocentric and all primary teachers know that educating a young child should start where the child is. Religious education aims to develop a child's understanding of him/herself, to recognize and reflect on personal strengths and weaknesses, likes and dislikes, loves and fears – these are the tools a child needs to understand his/her place in life, to cope with its joys and disappointments and to build positive self-esteem. As pupils progress through primary school this awareness of self develops. Children should be encouraged to reflect at the appropriate stage about their changing capacities and potentials, about those events which mark points throughout life, i.e. birth, initiation, marriage and death ceremonies, and about how these customs can mirror the emotions of the individual.

The National Curriculum documents specify the 'spiritual' dimension as an area in child education and development. Here, then, the 'spiritual' element can be identified within RE. This area will prepare the child as s/he addresses those ultimate' questions 'Who am I?', 'Why do I exist?', 'Who loves me?', 'What is life . . . and death?', 'What is beyond death?', and starts to understand his/her place in the world and to grapple with the meaning of existence. Here s/he is concerned about the spiritual side of life and encountering spirituality reflected in customs and rituals.

2. Relationships with Family, Friends, Community and the World

From an early age a child is aware of ways in which immediate family affect his or her well-being. If mum, dad, brother or sister don't meet the demands of the child, displeasure is experienced – if they do feed, change, play and comfort at appropriate moments, then generally a child is contented. With the early years of schooling a child's experiences become far broader. Not only do the immediate family affect the child, but school friends, teachers, doctors and others also play their part.

This area of 'relationships' has been identified as an important contributor to religious education, although clearly it is evident throughout school life and at home. Religious education aims to encourage reflection about the mutual responses between people, how relationships are significant in families, among friends and within the community and the world at large. Relationships affect self-esteem, identity and influence personal values and beliefs. Tolerance and respect for the needs, values and beliefs of those around should also be developed alongside a growing awareness of personal actions and their effects on others.

Here lies the groundwork for understanding the significance of community in religious life, how communities of faith function within a wider social setting, and how individuals find a place within that framework.

3. Responses to the Natural World

Humankind's fascination by the natural world is very evident when looking at religious phenomena. Stories, customs and rituals throughout history and within various cultures reflect the cycle of death and rebirth, the forces of nature, the creation of the world and the place of men and women within that pattern of nature. Here, then, is a vital area for well-balanced religious education. Children should be given opportunities to consider and respect the wonders and beauties of the natural world, and the immensity of the forces of nature – what influence do these have on human life and how do pupils respond?

Children from inner-city schools may not have some advantages of their 'country cousins' in rural schools, who may be more in touch with nature and more aware of the changing seasons. Urban schools will need to compensate by tending window-boxes, keeping pets in school, making a wildlife garden in the school grounds and so on. Pupils from urban schools, however, may be less likely to take the natural world for granted and might recognize the awesomeness of nature more readily. Alongside their own responses, older juniors (Key Stage 2) can investigate how others view the natural world by looking at creation myths and legends and at rituals and customs which respond to the awesomeness and the mystery of nature.

4. Understanding Religious Beliefs, Practices and Experiences

This last area is perhaps the one most easily identified as religious education. Children should be introduced to the nature of religious belief and the effects of commitment. They might begin to discover how men and women communicate religious ideas through art, gesture, music and writings, and how rituals express common feelings and beliefs. They can start to see how various faith communities embrace particular moral codes. Pupils can investigate various festivals, encountering stories, interpreting the symbolism and appreciating the significance to adherents. They might investigate religious leaders and start to understand their impact in history and today.

Now that we have identified what religious education can contribute to a primary curriculum, you may like to involve yourself in a task which will illustrate how opportunities for RE can be identified in a cross-curricular theme. If you have a colleague or colleagues with whom you can share your thoughts, this may be helpful.

1. Consider the theme 'Food' and list some key features of food and its significance in religious practice. Give yourselves about 4/5 minutes.

* * * * * *

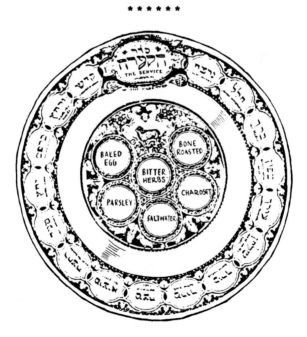

You may have included in your list: sharing, symbolism, enjoyment, distribution, abstinence. It is important to identify key features like these as an initial step.

2. Now list appropriate material which can be introduced to primary pupils which will enable them to encounter the key elements you have identified. There will be the 'implicit' dimension which is part of a child's own experience, and the 'explicit' dimension, the body of knowledge relating to food which is probably beyond the child's experience. (There is no need to work out a detailed teaching strategy for this exercise.)

3. Check your suggestions against the four main areas of religious education above (pp. 21–23) or against you local RE Agreed Syllabus. Note the links between the RE areas and your suggestions. Your check-list may look something like this:

Activity/Content	Key Elements	RE Area in Agreed Syllabus
birthday party	sharing symbolism enjoyment	awareness of self relationships with others
Passover or Easter	sharing symbolism enjoyment	relationships with others understanding beliefs, practices and experiences
Ramadan and Eid	abstinence sharing enjoyment	relationships with others understanding beliefs, practices and experiences

RE and the National Curriculum

Many teachers are already convinced of the importance of RE within the curriculum but the requirements of the Education Reform Act (1988) for the core and foundation subjects are demanding and time consuming. Understandably, many wonder how RE can possibly find a place in the busy school week. One way to tackle the problem, and meet the legal requirement to include RE in the curriculum, is to investigate cross-curricular links with other subject areas. This is done most easily within a thematic-based approach to the curriculum.

We have already looked at opportunities for RE for the theme 'Food'. Here are examples of other subject areas that could contribute to this theme. You may wish to check these out in National Curriculum guidelines.

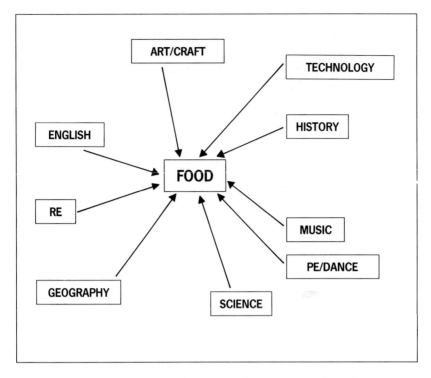

These are just a few examples and you may wish to investigate other subject areas, or perhaps you and your colleagues might like to develop another theme for RE and locate further links with National Curriculum guidelines. We hope you will feel reassured that RE and other areas of the curriculum can work in harmony together.

Attainment Targets for RE

Since the Education Reform Act, several bodies and groups have worked on suggestions for attainment targets in religious education (Westhill College, FARE, the RE Council, for example). There is no legislation for national RE attainment targets, but some LEAs have produced their own or modified those already published for use in their schools. SCAA has published model syllabuses as guidance for those LEAs which have not yet produced Agreed Syllabuses for RE. Attainment targets for RE become legally binding if they are adopted by the local SACRE (Standing Advisory Council for RE; see p. 8) and included in the LEA's Agreed Syllabus for RE.

If your LEA has adopted attainment targets for RE, check these against your suggestions for the religious dimension of the 'Food' theme, and see which attainment targets can be met by the theme.

There is a place for RE within today's primary curriculum, but its content must be carefully identified and planned precisely within coherent schemes of work to enable pupils' spiritual and religious development to flourish.

CHAPTER
6

THE THEMATIC APPROACH; THE SPIRAL CURRICULUM

Those who have been brought up on themes or topics might be hard pressed to provide reasons for what they do. Perhaps they should because there are teachers who see the National Curriculum pushing them back into subject-based teaching, despite the approval of the National Curriculum Council and inspectors mentioned in Chapter 1.

In this chapter we shall use the word 'theme' in its everyday sense (not in the sense of NCC themes such as Citizenship, Environment). Some teachers may still use the word 'topic' when referring to this approach.

Some popular arguments for using themes are:

1. It is the natural approach to learning; children and adults are normally interested in the age of Elizabeth, the Romans, Spain, or travel, rather than 'the history of . . .', 'the art of . . .'. It was only the grammar-school approach to learning that inflicted subjects on primary schools, with teachers having to teach about the Romans in history, Egypt in geography and David Livingstone's work in RE, for example.

2. It is less confusing than the approach which might require children to hold together the Romans, Egypt and Livingstone in their minds.

3. It is easier for the teacher to prepare for and resource. Books for use in the classroom do not usually put the subject-matter into watertight compartments. The teacher's precious time can be concentrated on one area of research rather than trying to find out about the disparate items mentioned above.

4. We can bring a variety of skills and approaches to bear on the same theme and this helps pupils to be aware of and understand the different ways of looking at things. For example, the geographer may want to look at the expanding horizons of the Elizabethans, the historian the perennial fears of an invasion, the literary minded the development of the theatre, and those interested in religion the Catholic–Protestant tensions and the conviction that each had of being right. Put together these aspects amount to a portrait; kept separate they are pieces in a jigsaw puzzle.

A popular example is 'Clothes'. Protective clothing can be the science/hygiene aspect, the kinds of clothes worn in certain historical times provide more than adequate scope for historical exploration, clothes and climate as well as sources of fabrics could be the geographical element, the special clothes worn by pilgrims to Makkah, Christian priests, Buddhist monks and Sikhs give ample opportunities for religious education. You may well be able to supply further ideas for art, music and literature as well as mathematics.

It might seem that themes can have no opponents. However there are critics. Some of their objections are as follows:

1. Withdrawal on grounds of conscience is difficult for teachers and children.

2. The integrity of the subject is lost in a great blur.

3. Subjects, especially religious education, can easily be neglected.

4. There is a danger of overkill – Elizabethan dress, food, language, music, art, science, medicine, punishments, . . . , as well as the things mentioned in 4 above!

5. The need to adopt a variety of stances and to help children to assume them too can cause problems. For example there are historical and religious reasons for the vestments worn by Christian priests and Sikhs. We have to realize that we get different answers depending on which questions we ask, historical or religious.

6. Children may study the same theme several times without any addition to content or learning new skills and concepts. The result is boring repetition.

How weighty do you consider these arguments to be with regard to religious education?

Each objection should be respected and taken seriously, though we would argue that they can all be met.

1. The right to withdraw   If the kind of RE which we advocate is accepted, withdrawal should become unnecessary. However, there is a PR job to be done. The teacher whose experience has been of having religion rammed down his or her throat will obviously object to doing the same and may only be persuaded slowly that the purpose of the subject has changed. It may be helpful if you take their class for RE to do something which is not Christian, display some artwork, and hopefully get them to the point of saying, 'Is that what you do in RE? I wouldn't mind doing that.' Of course, s/he will have to accept the Christianity element too, eventually, but to begin with it might maintain or strengthen the barriers, not remove them. It is important to win over these teachers because they have frequently so much to offer, besides the fact that their negative hostility can cause so much damage. There may still be some teachers who regard religion as superstitious nonsense. It will be much harder to persuade them that children have a right to study beliefs and values in such a way that they may, if they wish, be in a position to share or refute this view for themselves, and that to refuse to teach RE may be just as wrong as being eager to teach it for the purpose of evangelism.

2. The integrity of the subject can be lost in a great blur   It can also be lost if Hindu creation myths are told simply as stories of fantasy or Christmas is reduced to a moral exercise in caring and sharing combined with a show put on for parents. It all comes down to aims. If our purpose is to enable pupils to understand the place of religion in human life, or what it means to hold religious beliefs and values and to take them seriously, then we shall explore what Christmas means to Christians and the creation myths to Hindus and we shall go for exploring meaning not telling every myth that we can find or examining all the festivals of the major religions. The 'blur' effect seems to come from going for quantity and having no aims or the wrong ones. We do need to ask ourselves repeatedly whether the skills, attitudes and concepts as well as the content are enhancing an understanding of beliefs and values. The story of Noah or of David defeating Goliath can become nothing more than a folk tale. Because these stories come from the Bible they need not necessarily promote understanding. What do you consider to be their religious meaning?

3. Subjects can be neglected   To ensure that each curriculum area receives due attention, some schools require teachers to make a grid like a noughts-and-crosses board, mark in the areas involved in the topic and then fill in the history, religious education, science, . . . , allocation as a percentage. Religious education should have at least 5% given to it. In this way the neglect of any subject, accidental or intentional, can be seen at a glance. Neglect is a matter of attitude, not method! The Dearing Report states that RE should receive the same time allocation as such subjects as history, geography and technology.

4. Overkill can be as harmful as neglect, though it is a rarer disease and one we would prefer to encounter if we must make a choice! It is usually related to a desire to include material from every religious tradition and to go for content instead of skills, concepts and attitudes. If we could persuade ourselves to produce a set of criteria for deciding what examples best illustrate some concept, for example worship, we might then be selective not exhaustive. Buddhist meditation, prayer in the mosque, and a Methodist morning service might be our choice. Of course, this would not prevent those children who have different experiences of worship sharing them with us, but it does enable some probing to be made towards a consideration of what worship is and a recognition of the diversity of responses to worshipping. Some pupils may ask why people worship but that is really a question for the teacher to raise at Key Stage 4.

Selection may not be possible in a multifaith school (see also Chapter 9) but we hope that older classes might be persuaded that they do not need to cover every tradition in every topic. However, if we acknowledge a legal requirement always to include Christianity we cannot in all fairness exclude other faiths which may be represented in the class in larger numbers!

One other reason for overkill is the amount of time given to the theme. Half a term is usually enough, with infants perhaps only four weeks.

5. The need to adopt a variety of stances hasn't really anything to do with the thematic approach. Even if history and religion are studied separately the teacher and the children still need to recognize that each discipline requires a different stance. If we look at the food which people in the Middle Ages enjoyed at Christmas we shall be concerned about availability and the fashions of the day. But in RE the emphasis will be on what the celebration meant to them as well as on *how* they observed the religious festival. With Pesach (Passover), the historical approach might be to examine the Exodus account of the deliverance from Egypt. The RE aspect is the way in which Jews keep the festival and what it *means* to them now.

6. Repetition is also the result of not method so much a lack of liaison between the various teachers in a school. The Romans or the Good Samaritan might be covered two or three times between Key Stages 1 and 4. but there must be development. In the past there seldom was. Perhaps the introduction of attainment targets in RE will encourage spiral growth in RE as well as science and mathematics.

Planning a Theme: 'Water'

Once the focus of interest has been decided in consultation with the school co-ordinator who is responsible for avoiding duplications, omissions and failures to consider the National Curriculum, the usual approach is to produce a web diagram with the focus at the centre and subject areas leading from it. We have chosen 'Water' as an example.

This theme would be chosen for a number of reasons.

- The general importance of water. It is essential for life.
- It invites exploration through a large number of curriculum areas.
- Its use in religious practices is something which primary children should be capable of examining.
- It meets the kinds of attainment targets which various bodies in religious education are recommending, for example:

From *Attainment in RE. A Handbook for Teachers,* Westhill College, Birmingham, 1989

AT 5: Belief and Identity

Key Stage 1   (b) be able to talk about some features of a ceremony in which young children are welcomed into a faith community

Key Stage 2   (d) be able to describe in outline a ceremony associated with joining or belonging to a religious community

AT 6: The Natural World

Key Stage 1   (a) be familiar with some appropriate stories from various traditions about human experiences of the natural world

(b) begin to be aware that human beings are dependent on the earth's resources, and be familiar with some expressions of gratitude for the products of the earth

Key Stage 2   (d) be familiar with ceremonies, including religious ceremonies, which mark transition in the human life cycle

AT 9: Expressing Meaning

Key Stage 1   (a) begin to recognise examples of symbolic actions, gestures, dress and artefacts and be able to talk about some of their possible meanings

Key Stage 2   (a) be able to use the word 'symbol' correctly and give appropriate examples

(d) be able to identify meanings expressed through art, music, movement and drama, and recognise ways in which these media are used in religion to express meaning

Key Stage 3   (a) be able to interpret meanings from examples of rituals, artefacts, art and music, including religious examples

From *A FARE Deal for RE*, Exeter University School of Education, 1990

Key Stage 1

AT 5: Religious Practice **5.** Pupils should know some features of a ceremony in which young children are welcomed into a religious group

Key Stage 2

AT 5: Religious Practice **4.** Pupils should be aware that within the course of many believers' lives there are special customs and ceremonies marking important moments in life and in the year's cycle

AT 6: Religious Language **2.** Pupils should know some examples of religious symbolism

3. Pupils should know that a variety of means of communication is used in religion to express meaning

The implicit RE would focus on the importance of water and our everyday use of and dependence on it. As a result, we hope, children would realize that it is natural for religions to use water in many of their practices.

Our aims in terms of explicit religion would be to examine how water is used in some religions and to begin to discover why. Examples would be Christian baptism and bathing in the River Ganges. Wuzu before prayers in Islam could also be included as well as the use of amrit in Sikh initiation or perhaps the mikvah in Judaism. A bath is customary for Hindus and Sikhs before going to a mandir or gurdwara.

The story of Noah, the Israelites crossing the Sea of Reeds (popularly the Red Sea), or flood narratives in Hinduism and some other religions would not be used because they don't really have anything to do with water as they stand, though they may well indicate concern about the power of the elements in people of long ago. (See section on 'The Bible in RE', p. 60, for further discussion on this point.)

Before reaching the religious aspects we would want to look at special times when children have a good wash, before going to a party or to Gran's, perhaps, or washing their hands before handling their parents' photograph album, or a stamp collection. Here we come across reasons which have to do not only with physical cleanliness but with the significance of the deed to be done or the thing to be handled. This leads some way towards religious usages.

Other curriculum areas might look at the importance of water for sustaining life (science), distribution relating to climate and effect on land formation (geography) or effects of pollution (geography). History might examine some voyages of exploration or the water supply in Roman times.

Cross-curricular Links with the Theme 'Water'

WATER

Properties of water

Aquatic life

Designing, creating and tending a wild-life garden

Life sustaining

Water cycle

Water supply in Roman times

Distribution relating to climate

Designing a water-powered device

Water and land formation

English
listening
reading
speaking
writing

Creating pictures of water in different moods

Symbolic use of water in religious rituals

Batik, tie-dye, etc.

Capacity

Reflecting on life's dependence on water

In RE we would be taking up the idea of washing to make clean symbolically. The baby will have been well scrubbed before being taken to church for baptism, but now water is used to show renewal. The Ganges, on the other hand, is a dirty river, at Varanasi anyway, but pilgrims believe that they are made pure by bathing in it. Pontius Pilatus used water symbolically to demonstrate that he was not responsible for Jesus' death. This is rather different but might be used nevertheless. Is the story of Jesus washing the feet of his disciples about water symbolism? Only if his words, 'Unless I wash you, you have no part with me,' (John 13:8) are explored, then it might be associated with the membership rite of baptism, otherwise it becomes a lesson in humility. Ultimately, the use of water in rituals has usually to do with inner spiritual pollution and purification but these are difficult concepts to comprehend, as we sometimes find when working with undergraduates. In the primary school we can scarcely begin probing towards them, but it is good for the teacher to understand the concepts which lie at the end of the process.

The following boxes provide suggestions for activities which can introduce pupils to some of the RE content mentioned here. They are presented in three key stages in order to illustrate how the theme can be developed, building on previous knowledge and understanding as pupils progress through school.

Key Stage 1

Aim
- To help pupils begin to understand life's dependence on water.
- To help pupils begin to appreciate that water is used in a variety of ways.

Suggested Activities
- Grow cress seeds watering some but not others. Keep a chart of their growth. (Make sure it's a fair test.)
- Devise a watering rota for the class plants.
- Keep a chart of all the times during the day when the pupils use water.
- Go for a walk in the rain. On return think of some 'watery' words and produce a class poem.
- Discuss and produce a frieze showing all the washing rituals of the class with written explanations underneath. (E.g. Thomas washes his hair every Friday, Jane has a shower before she goes to a party, William washes his hands before he looks at the photograph album.)

- Take the pupils to a local church/chapel and show them the font/baptismal tank (or provide photographs). Ask them to speculate on its use.
- Ask a vicar to role-play a baptism with a doll for the pupils.
- Role-play a Sikh baby-naming ceremony.

Key Stage 2

Aim
- To help pupils recognize the qualities of water and begin to understand its use in religious rituals.

Suggested Activities
- In groups, brainstorm the word 'water' considering its qualities and uses. Display the results for all the groups to compare.
- Collect as a class a wide variety of pictures showing water in many moods and being used in a variety of ways including religious rituals. Produce a large collage.
- Produce a display of items which are important in Christian baptism. Investigate the significance of the ritual through looking at cards, prayers and the words used in baptism services.
- Investigate and role-play or produce a collage of John the Baptist baptizing Jesus.
- Show slides/videos/posters of Hindus washing in the River Ganges. Notice the expressions on the people's faces. How do they look? What do the children think the ritual means to them?
- Tell the story of the River Ganges (the Goddess Ganga).
- Investigate and produce diagrams showing wuzu (ritual ablutions) in preparation for Muslim prayer. Consider why this preparatory wash is important to Muslims.
- Encourage pupils to reflect on and share their thoughts about special occasions when they would wash in preparation.

Key Stage 3

Aim
- To help pupils understand the symbolic nature of water and its significance to members of various faith communities.

Suggested Activities
- Investigate in groups a variety of religious rituals using water:

child baptism ⎫	amrit ceremony	(Sikh)
adult baptism ⎬ (Christian)	washing in Ganges	(Hindu)
holy water ⎭	lantern ceremony	(Buddhist)
wuzu (Muslim)	ritual washing	(Jewish)

Each group then organizes a presentation of artwork, drama, narration, etc., to share their findings with their classmates. They should pay particular attention to the *purpose* of the ritual and how it makes the adherent feel.
- Invite in members of a faith community (perhaps a vicar or an imam) to demonstrate and explain the significance of water in their religious rituals. Prepare pupils to ask informed questions.

Skills, Attitudes and Concepts in Religious Education

Religious education which is concerned only with content is inadequate for a number of reasons. It is likely to concentrate on facts which, though they must be known, are not significant in themselves. Britain went to war with Germany in September 1939 is a fact, but why this happened is more important, and that includes understanding how Germany could come to give power to Hitler. What to look for in a church is dealt with in a number of books, but they seldom include looking for the congregation and asking why they go. Such education demands the acquisition of skills, the ability to question and develop certain attitudes to what is being studied, and the understanding of concepts like national pride in history or worship in RE.

The exclusively content-based approach is not only undesirable but impossible. There is so much of it. Each year archaeologists discover so much about Roman Britain that only the specialist can find time to cope with the literature, and the Romans haven't been doing much in Britain for some time! The religious-studies teacher who tries to cover six religions in every topic has no chance of achieving much. The solution is to recognize that content should be illustrative rather than dominant. So Lourdes and the Hajj might be religious examples in a topic on journeys and would be used to examine why some people make pilgrimages. A topic on communities might look at the life and contributions of Christian nuns and Buddhist monks.

Few skills and attitudes, if any, are specific to the study of religion but no other curriculum area is likely to concern itself with such things as worship, prayer, ritual, beliefs, and meaning (see table below). We can begin to examine these in the primary school. Regarding content, however, we are providing pieces of a jigsaw which is not yet complete; many bits are still missing. Regarding skills, attitudes and concepts, we are beginning the process of developing them. We must trust our secondary-school colleagues to continue and complete the task.

Skills and/or Attitudes	Concepts
• Willingness to see and listen without wishing to judge	• Faith/belief
• Readiness to share the experiences and ideas of others	• Worship
• Guided imagination	• Prayer
• Expression of thoughts and feelings	• Meditation
• Curiosity and skills of investigation	• Meaning
• Use of religious language	• Ritual
• Evaluation of evidence	• Religion
• Awareness of one's own prejudices	• Ethics/morality
• Respect for oneself and others	• Commitment
• Promotion of positive attitudes towards understanding beliefs and values	• Myth
	• What it means to belong to a faith community

A Closer Look at 'Food'

You may already have explored 'Food' in the exercise suggested on p. 23. We shall now examine the theme in more detail, stressing continuity and progression as well as the implicit and explicit elements.

With the youngest children we might be encouraging them to think about favourite foods and why they like them, about parties, why they have them and how they decide who to invite. Through these questions they would be exploring the idea that food has symbolic significance, though the word 'symbol' would not be used. There is more to food than healthy or unhealthy eating, and the children should begin to become aware that meals bind people together. Explicit religious material could be the story of Jesus eating a meal with his friends (the Last Supper, though we would omit any reference to the betrayal or 'This is my body/blood'), parts of the Seder (Passover) meal, and other celebrations such as Eid.

Top infants and juniors might be taken to a church to experience a simulated communion service conducted by the friendly neighbourhood minister. Here again mention would be made of the meal Jesus shared with his friends and his command 'Do this in memory of me', but the emphasis would be shifted to a meal which Christians share together. One reason for its simplicity is that St Paul came across Christians who were turning the meal into something divisive, bringing their 'Fortnum and Mason' hampers and vintage wine while others had only stale bread to eat. The body and blood symbolism is still for the future. The point to be explored is the Christian family sharing a simple meal around a common table. In some churches this unity is demonstrated by drinking from a single cup and breaking a portion of bread from a single loaf.

The Jewish meal at the beginning of Shabbat (the Sabbath) could also be simulated, again the emphasis being on the idea of a family, some of whose members may travel many miles to be together for Shabbat. Some children may want to discuss similarities with Christian communion services and so realize more fully the way food is used in very much the same way in different religions and cultures. Some teachers and parents may feel sensitive about the use of simulation in religious education. This matter is considered further on p. 69.

Top junior/middle is the stage to examine the way in which food can distinguish one group of people from another. Thus the dietary rules in Judaism and Islam would be considered especially, but also the requirement to be a church member or 'love the Lord Jesus' as a condition of communion and to accept the caste-rejecting teachings of Sikhism if one is to share langar. Kosher and hallal rules should be explained not through some attempt at rationalizing them but in terms of inclusiveness and exclusiveness and obedience. If you are a Muslim, for example, you refrain from eating pork or drinking alcohol because you believe God has provided you with a way of discipline and obedience which entails avoiding them. If food prohibitions seem strange and stupid one might consider the British attitude to eating horse or dog! Vegetarianism is another dimension of food in religion which might be introduced at this stage.

Do All Themes Have Opportunities for RE?

Sometimes RE may have only a peripheral place in a theme or none at all. Far better to exclude it altogether than forge links which are not natural, for example by working on cubits and spans in a topic on measuring, arguing that they are mentioned in the Bible. Time could be spent on consolidating something else, in the same way that if geography could not be included in a theme on Christmas time might be given to learning how to use an atlas. A mini RE topic might be aimed at helping children to find their way around the Bible, looking at the local mosque or church, or assembling a detailed portrait of Jesus, Guru Nanak or the Buddha. It could be a time for consolidation. However, it is preferable to be able to keep RE within the thematic framework and the way to do this is to discuss your theme as a group rather then decide on its title and then force the maths, geography and RE into it.

An example might be 'The Vikings'. As people interested in history and geography we could warm to this suggestion, but where would the RE come in? The fascinating stories of St Cuthbert's body being carried round the north of England and eventually coming to rest at Durham, and the remarkable preservation of the Lindisfarne Gospels are magnificent and could be explored for their religious rather than legendary historical significance. The stories do raise interesting questions about the power of relics and the reasons for choosing particular sites as places to erect religious buildings. We might be tempted to look at the work of missionaries among the Vikings and enter into the debate which must have taken place when, for example, Harold Bluetooth of Denmark decided to embrace the Christian faith and require all his subjects to do likewise.

If we are really going to include religious education in a topic on the Vikings we need to consider how they saw the world. As they put out to sea in their longships what beliefs helped them face the unseen dangers? What values did they cherish? What festivals did they celebrate, how, and why? We may find out that they were more sophisticated spiritually than the Christian monk who wrote about the 'fury of the norsemen' would have us believe. And, of course, we will not refer to them as 'pagans' or their beliefs as 'superstitions'. Neither of these words has a place in religious education. (We tend to use them pejoratively about the beliefs and practices of others but would be insulted if our own cherished ideas were spoken of in this way.)

All this could be done, but we might want to confine our religious education to contemporary religions and ask, therefore, that the topic might be 'Journeys', which would not deprive the historian of studying the Vikings but would allow religious education to focus on pilgrimage. This solution might be acceptable once but as the whole of Britain's history is either the story of journeys which brought migrants here or the account of the migrants who have made up the 'British race' going elsewhere, the work of colonizers and missionaries, it is one that should not be used too often. 'Journeys' is a good example to work on in terms of covering Key Stages 1, 2 and 3.

The examples in this chapter indicate how some kind of developmental approach to religious education might be made and the need, therefore, for someone to co-ordinate the RE/thematic programme of the school. The following themes are popular in primary schools because they can be explored across the curriculum at various levels and fit into the experiential world of the children and/or the National Curriculum. You might like to consider a three- or at least two-stage approach to RE within some of them.

Signs and Symbols   Hands   Light   Beginnings   Journeys   The Romans   Clothes

The Environment   Buildings   Families   Books   Celebration   Migration

RELIGIOUS EDUCATION AND MORAL EDUCATION

The scene is a meeting of teachers and governors, including parent-governors, at Downhill Primary School. The issue is a complaint of shop-lifting made by a local newsagent to which a parent adds the charge that her nine-year-old is being bullied by children in the fourth year.

'Downhill is certainly going downhill,' says the chairperson, 'what are we going to do?'

'Not make jokes of that kind,' is one response and some blame is attached to the shopkeeper for having open shelves, but gradually the teachers are able to raise the question of what kind of school everyone wants in terms of human relationships, attitudes and behaviour.

You might like to discuss what kind of school you want to work in or develop. Is it one with rules imposed from above by the headteacher and presumably the governors? Is it one where pupils are involved in the discussion and implementation of a policy which they have actually helped formulate? (We know of schools at both extremes and many in between, and are aware of others where there seems to be no policy, so there are no real guidelines for children or teachers to use.)

The school formulated a policy which included phrases such as 'respect for one another and those who live in the neighbourhood of the school', 'care for the environment', 'being honest', 'caring for one another, especially those younger than ourselves and the elderly in the community'.

At a teachers' meeting the headteacher asked those responsible for each subject area what contribution they could make to inculcating these high ideals and turning them into basic day-to-day realities. It came to them as a shock. One or two began to bluster their way out be saying, 'When we do the RE part of our topic we look at caring for one another. You know . . . if I'm looking at water in science I might talk about Christian Aid or Oxfam helping people to dig wells in Africa or India . . . and perhaps not wasting water in this country.'

Pat, the teacher responsible for RE, was not at all pleased with this reply.

Can you think why? Before reading further can you suggest what objections s/he might have made?

Eventually Pat made two points. One was that RE was not just about caring and sharing. If they came to her/him to discuss the RE aspect of a topic on water s/he would be talking about simulating a baptism, or bathing in the River Ganges, and the symbolism behind these activities. How would they like it if s/he made the science part of their water topic caring for Indians by digging wells? (Murmurs of 'National Curriculum' and 'Science is different, it has to do with knowledge.')

Then Pat added the point that RE too had a body of knowledge, and also skills, attitudes and concepts to work with. It wasn't about changing attitudes and making children kind and good any more than any other part of the curriculum.

Mrs Oxtoby, the headteacher, called for order. She asked her colleagues to reflect on what they were doing if they made moral concerns part of RE only. They were suggesting that values were the exclusive property of religion. As a Humanist she resented that inference. She couldn't endorse the view that only religious people cared! They were also reducing religion to a code of behaviour. Though she was not a religious person she had her beliefs and her morality came from them, not the other way round. Was it right to impose religiously based morals on children who, they knew, came from homes which were not religious? She had needed no priming by Pat, who was pleased to hear her comments. They carried more weight coming from her!

The head then went on, 'I'd like you all to think what your subject area might contribute to implementing our social policy statement. And that includes you, Pat. RE isn't going to wriggle out of sharing altogether!'

You might like to write a hundred-word statement on what contribution your specialism might make in these circumstances. Discuss it with people with other subject interests.

Pat came up with some don'ts as well as does:

- *Don't moralize. We all hated it as children and switched off so why do we think we can be more persuasive preachers than our own teachers were?*
- *Don't appeal to the Bible or Jesus, or even the Qur'an. The children may not be religious believers who respect their authority. (Like the boy who said, 'I'm not a Christian so I can steal if I like!')*
- *Don't forget that even if religiously based moral principles don't change, practical expressions of them do. For example, the New Testament doesn't condemn slavery and for centuries Christians took part in the slave trade, but today no Christian would endorse slavery. We mustn't imply that values are always static. Religions and societies are dynamic, constantly changing, if they are living. If they cease to change they soon die.*

More positively, Pat thought that children could look at the way religions, like other organizations, have rules of membership and the reasons for them. There was the Khalsa code in Sikhism, the four Muslim pillars which are the practical consequence of belief in the first pillar, the promises which Christians make at various times, and why these kinds of rules are needed just as much as the safety rules on the road or in scientific investigation. There could be a cross-curricular theme or mini-topic on 'rules' or on how the class would live if it was stranded on a desert island. Often, though, conduct would be covered when examining the festival of Baisakhi (celebrating the founding of the Khalsa), or fasting in Islam, or Lent in Christianity, for example. 'Commitment', Pat felt, was probably the key word. Religious rules are a way of showing commitment. They relate to God as well as to other human beings. Being kind and good is not the whole religious story, as Shabbat (the Jewish Sabbath) and Lent demonstrate, for example. Primarily they are ways through which Jews or Christians express their devotion and obedience to God.

If you had been confronted by Mrs Oxtoby what would your RE response have been?

For further reading see *Spiritual and Moral Development – A Discussion Paper* (National Curriculum Council, April 1993).

CHAPTER
8

TEACHING CHRISTIANITY

'I find Christianity the most difficult religion to teach' is an observation commonly made at INSET courses. Reasons for this statement and state of affairs vary but the reality is that Christianity is often neglected not in favour of other religions as some suppose, but to be replaced by moralistic encouragement to be kind and good, sharing and caring. When it is taught the emphasis is still generally on biblical stories.

You might like to suggest reasons of your own why Christianity seems to be so hard to teach, discuss them with colleagues and then compare them with ours.

One has to do with tradition. Religious education in the experience of most people over the age of forty was a form of nurture. Britain was considered to be a Christian country, its teachers Christian and its children Christians in the making. Leaving aside the presence of Islam and other faiths in the Britain of today, a red herring often excusing the non-existence of RE, the fact is that society has changed. Teachers are no more likely to be Christian than are bus drivers, dentists, or nurses. One in five, or less, is what we could expect if we could find an average school to visit. This means that most primary-school teachers, if they still think that their task is to nurture children in the Christian faith, believe that they are being asked to engage in an act of hypocrisy. No wonder they have replaced religious education with a sort of moralizing which is broadly but not explicitly Christian and some children reach secondary school with little Christian knowledge, even of the meaning of Christmas.

The concern not to be hypocritical, which has been mentioned elsewhere, is particularly important in the context of teaching Christianity. Some Christians still believe that it is their duty to witness to their faith in the classroom and transmit their faith to pupils. A consequence of this is an unease among teachers who cannot in all conscience do that. The argument goes like this: if it is the duty of teachers to nurture children in the Christian faith, the non-Christian cannot teach RE. Inevitably, then, there must be only a minority of primary teachers who can teach it.

Paradoxically, therefore, it may actually be those Christians who want to nurture or evangelize who are responsible to some extent for the lack of religious education in some classrooms! They have given eighty per cent of the primary teaching force the impression that they cannot teach it. This is certainly likely to be the case if a teacher is negatively disposed to Christianity as a small number of teachers are. They may have difficulty teaching it in an open though positive way, as they would hope to teach other aspects of the curriculum. The difficulty is not so much teaching Christianity as detaching oneself from the notion that the purpose is nurture. It is not. It is to help children *understand* what it means to be a Christian in terms of belief and practice. The vast majority of teachers will adopt the open approach once they are aware of it.

Where there is some RE the emphasis, as we have said, seems to be on Bible stories. Teachers may have several reasons for telling them. They may be what they know, and can therefore teach, stories they heard when they were children. The teacher may be reassured by telling them, feeling that s/he has done some RE. Those parents who make the headlines of national newspapers by criticizing multifaith RE will be happy. They will not create a fuss! Christianity is being taught. But is it? Very often the story is divorced from its religious meaning and told merely as an example of kindness (healing miracles), friendship (Jesus and the disciples), or sharing (the boy's gesture at the Feeding of the Five Thousand). The use of the Bible is discussed in Chapter 10. At this point we confine ourselves to asking whether, when we use biblical material, we are conveying its religious message and challenge, only part of which has to do with loving our neighbour. As with good jokes so with Bible stories, it's the way you tell 'em that matters!

Resources

If teachers overcome the hurdles mentioned above, and accept the kinds of aims which are advocated in this book and by most specialists in religious education, they may have difficulty in finding suitable materials because:

- Most books on Christianity still seem to expect the reader already to have a knowledge of the faith which we would not expect in a book on Hinduism, for example.
- They are often written from faith to faith, by believers who suppose that the reader is a believer. They ask, for example, 'How do *you* observe Lent?' Not only does this assume that the reader is a Christian, it implies that they belong to a Lent-observing denomination!
- They are likely to be biblical. Even if the teacher has responded to new thinking about RE and sees the responsibility as being that of helping children to understand Christianity and what it means to be a Christian in terms of belief and practice, the back-up material is likely to be inadequate and geared to the old aim of nurture through Bible stories presented in seductively attractive story-books.

Lack of training + inadequate resources = no confidence

This equation provides the final reason for teachers avoiding Christianity. The resources for teaching other world religions are often far superior, and attention does not focus on the teacher's own beliefs.

The primary-school teacher has usually to carry the whole curriculum on her/his shoulders with only a ten to fifteen hour course in teaching each of the compulsory subjects, though mathematics, language and reading, and science usually fare much better. At the time of writing LMS seems to be killing off much INSET work in the aesthetic and humanities areas of the curriculum, so that curriculum development in them will be stunted unless teachers resort to using written materials like this book and those listed in the Resources section. However, books are no substitute for the human interaction which INSET courses should provide.

Stance is as important in religious education as it is in golf and cricket.

We as teachers, and the books we choose should be using the phrase 'Christians do this', or 'Christians believe . . .', not 'When we go to church . . .'. Not only is the use of 'we' an infringement of the integrity of the child who may not have made up her/his mind, it also endorses the heresy that being British is being Christian. This is untrue of a religion which emphasizes personal belief and commitment. It also adds to our problems when we are attempting to help children understand what it actually means to be a practising Christian. We shudder to think what a Muslim child might conclude about the nature of Christianity as he looks at British society as a whole and is invited to regard it as Christian, especially if he lives in an area of racist attacks (mostly by whites) or prostitution (mostly between white women and white men). Little wonder Christianity is often equated with permissiveness.

Teachers have never taught Christianity. We have confined ourselves to the Bible, which is not the same thing, and some stories of great Christians, with an element of theology for bright sixth-formers. Only recently a group of undergraduates in religious studies was asked if any of them had visited a church as part of their RE courses. Only two had, yet out of the thirty all but three had 'O' level or CSE and fifteen had done 'A' level, all in biblical studies.

They knew nothing about Christian worship, even why Sunday is a special day. They were not an unusual group in any respect. There is a need now to teach Christianity as we teach other faiths, with the same methods, aims, and assumptions of ignorance, and covering all its aspects.

You might like to discover where *your* children are in their knowledge and understanding of Christianity. If you simply ask them, 'Which of you is a Christian?', you may get some funny answers, like 'I'm a Catholic' or 'My gran's a Christian but my mum's a Baptist!'. It may be better to put up pictures on the wall showing local churches, both outside and inside, and seeing if any of the class can tell you anything about them. Children identify better with what they do than with abstractions. Perhaps we still need to be convinced that our children come to school as irreligiate as they are illiterate and innumerate. Perhaps this kind of exercise will persuade us.

Talking to teachers in secondary schools, we are led to conclude that children generally know little more about Christianity by the time they transfer, despite an annual diet of Christmas, if nothing else. It is no good beginning with Christianity *because* it is part of their experience. It is not. We must begin with their human experience, exploring it, enriching it, thinking about it, and then embark upon the task of helping children understand Christianity.

If we are prepared to teach Christianity in a rounded way, including using the Bible to some extent, what Christian material is suitable for use in primary schools? Here are some suggestions. Remember that your choice of content should enable children to develop the skills, attitudes and concepts listed in Chapter 6 (p. 34).

Aspects of Christianity

Jesus
- calling the fishermen disciples, meeting Zacchaeus, Palm Sunday, washing the disciples' feet, the Last Supper, the arrest, the story of the death and resurrection of Jesus told from Peter's point of view (older juniors);
- some aspects of the birth narratives;
- perhaps some parables, e.g. 'The Lost Coin', 'The Lost Sheep'; the aim, however, should be to bring out the importance of Jesus for Christians, at a level which children can appreciate.

Paul's story   some interesting episodes which bring out his commitment to Jesus, especially in a topic on the Romans. He is probably the best-known Roman citizen with the exception of a few emperors.

Worship   the church as a building and as a community of believers, studying and perhaps learning some hymns and prayers including the Lord's Prayer.

Baptism   emphasizing joining the Christian family.

Holy Communion   the Christian family meal (link with the story of the Last Supper).

Weddings

(All three rites above might be simulated, perhaps with the help of a friendly neighbourhood clergy person – why should it always be a man?)

Clergy, monks and nuns   especially as guests in school or hosts in their places of work.

The Bible   its place in worship, a book about Jesus, kinds of literature, stories of its growth (e.g. Paul's Letter to Philemon, Mark writing his Gospel), and of such men as Tyndale (but beware of raking over the dying fires of sectarianism).

Christian symbols   e.g. fish, lamb, cross.

Festivals   mainly Christmas and Easter:
- how they are celebrated;
- the stories Christians tell at them;
- what they mean to Christians.

Some stories about Christians   as up to date as possible, and take care in handling imperialistic missionary material which suggests that they civilized the savages! Care should be taken to avoid conveying the white, male stereotype.

The Old Testament would be treated as the Jewish Bible and not used in the Christianity sections of the syllabus. Teachers should, of course, be sensitive in handling material on the Jews generally and the Pharisees in particular (Jesus may well have been one!) and avoid conveying the idea that the Jews were responsible for the death of Jesus.

This list of suitable Christian material is surely adequate to ensure that children have been given a sound grounding in the religion before they enter secondary school. This content also lends itself to a variety of active learning approaches.

You might like to consider approaches and activities which could be used as well as themes in which these aspects of Christianity might be included. (Some of these will be discussed in Chapters 10–15 under 'Stories', 'Festivals' etc.)

It is the **beliefs** of a religion which are of ultimate importance. Some people may go to church for the music or fellowship, or to cope with personal loneliness, but in the long run it is the faith which enables one to live and to die which matters. Young children cannot understand doctrinal concepts and, it can be argued, do not have religious needs. It is to a human parent, teacher, or friend they turn for reassurance, not a heavenly father or Jesus. In the primary classroom beliefs or doctrines can and should be pointed to but not stressed, and probed towards through links with the children's own experience. For example, at Christmas and on other festival occasions, the importance of Jesus for Christians should come out as we consider why they remember the birth of someone who lived two thousand years ago, but the theology of the incarnation lies years ahead.

One teacher, after trying out some of the things suggested in this chapter and using active learning approaches, confessed to having enjoyed teaching RE for the first time in her career. In fact, she said, there was a danger of it taking over the timetable. Perhaps we shouldn't encourage that (though why not if science does!) but we hope we have convinced someone that teaching Christianity in the classroom can be rewarding and fun.

For further information on areas of Christianity to explore, see the suggestions in *Model Syllabuses for Religious Education Consultation Document* (SCAA, January 1994). (The address of SCAA is Newcombe House, 45 Notting Hill Gate, London W11 3JB.)

CHAPTER
9

THE SAME MULTIFAITH BALANCE FOR ALL?

Consider a class of white children, then a class of pupils representing several races. Imagine yourself entering those two classrooms. Would you expect to find the same RE content in each?

The answer is probably not, unless it were Christmas time! Why not? Can we list a few reasons why RE should differ in the two schools?

- Probably there are few Christians and many children of other faiths in the multifaith school.
- Perhaps the parents, governors and headteacher in the traditional school demand more Christianity than they would in the other.

Let us pause for a moment and consider how valid these reasons may actually be.

The traditional school may well have very few Christian families associated with it. Even Anglican denominational schools in the shire counties are often aware that Christian affiliation of any sort is limited to a minority of their families. (This is much less true of Roman Catholic schools.) In such areas as rural West Sussex and Yorkshire schools are pluralistic institutions but we may not realize it because everyone is white skinned. We may even take it for granted that children in these schools possess an almost innate knowledge of religion. This is not usually the case. There is a need to ensure that their religious education explores the beliefs and practices upon which such values as caring and sharing are based. An awareness of Christianity cannot be assumed.

Here our two schools may be at one, for different reasons. The traditional may steer clear of Christianity because the teacher is not a believer, knows the children's families are not and doesn't want to be accused of 'indoctrination'. In the multifaith school the fear is of seeming to be a missionary. In such bad examples we may find very little difference, very little identifiable religious education in either! Well-planned religious education should be a vital part of the curriculum in both kinds of school.

The demands of some Christian parents, but by no means all, for Christian RE can be just as strong in multifaith schools as in others, probably because they see the apparent erosion of traditional values. Perhaps the legacy of Empire, for them, has been the acceptance of the view that the world's other races are inferior. They may blame inner-city decay on the one factor that they can identify, demographic change, and react through the one school subject that seems to provide them with an opportunity to do so, RE.

What we are arguing is that circumstances are really not so different in the two types of school. Hopefully the overall aim of RE is the same. Each school is subject to the same Education Act and should also be responding positively to the sentence in DES Circular 3/89 which reads:

> The Government believes that all those concerned with religious education should seek to ensure that it promotes respect, understanding and tolerance for those who adhere to different faiths (para 8, page 5),

as well as to the injunction in the Act to:

> ... reflect the fact that the religious traditions in Great Britain are in the main Christian whilst taking account of the teaching and practices of the other principal religions represented in Great Britain (Ch. 40, part I, section 8).

The whole of the latter sentence is to be taken seriously, not just the 'in the main Christian' clause, or for that matter, 'taking account of the other principal religions'!

Another important similarity is that all British schools are preparing children to live in the same world. Changing patterns of employment, regional unemployment, and housing costs often mean that young people must leave the places where they were brought up in order to find work. They may end up not in the inner cities but probably in other urban areas where they will come across and work with men and women of other ethnic and religious groups. Even if the encounter is going to be no more than meeting a black clippy at Victoria station or on the underground, though it may be receiving treatment from a Sikh doctor in mid Wales, they need to be able to value that person as a human being, to have a concept of 'normal' which includes them, and not to be alarmed, as some children still are. Not too long ago a boy from Hampshire went to London to take part in an athletics meeting. On his return he told his teacher of his shock at seeing boys who were black. (The effect was to convert her to multicultural education.)

The planners, politicians, and others whose decisions determine the future of our inner cities were not raised there and tend not to live there. They are to be found in the shire counties or the rural parts of Warwickshire, Yorkshire, or Berkshire and the stockbroker belt of Surrey. Their children will wield a similar influence in the same kinds of occupation. They need to be educated to understand the beliefs and values of the people for whose welfare they will be responsible though they may never actually meet them.

There are, then, as many practical arguments for traditional schools teaching Islam as there are for Muslims in Tower Hamlets learning something about Christianity, as well as the fact that the law, in the form of Agreed Syllabuses, does not permit an exclusively Christian diet to be given.

Method and Approach

It is at the point of teaching that differences might seem most valid, but here again we might pause for a moment. If we begin where the children are, where are they in terms of religion?

In a rural school or market town we might assume a Christian reference point, but, as we have suggested, there may really be none at all in the children's own lives and experience. Also, we could be facing the hidden problem of parental indifference or hostility to Christianity (see Chapter 8). There is much to be said for finding out where the children are before we teach them any RE at all. After all that is what we do in number, and then we begin with experience.

However, we will concede that for most teachers in an infant school along the south coast it will be right to begin with Christianity; we ask only that they make a *conscious* decision to do so, rather than follow the practice of earlier generations, and *without* assumptions of innate knowledge.

In the multifaith school children and parents from religious minorities may be reassured by an approach to religious education which immediately recognizes the worth of their traditions. In these schools there is a cultural richness which teachers elsewhere often envy. By acknowledging it practically right from the start, the goodwill of the local communities can be won with beneficial results which range from positive attitudes to education on the part of the children to a readiness to lend artefacts and give financial as well as moral support for the assistance which the school is trying to give their children. The understandable alarm suffered by parents who see school as a threat to the language, culture, values, and beliefs which they cherish can be replaced by a confidence based on trust. Schools have always been receptive in human terms of friendship and kindness towards the children who come to them, now, to an increasing extent, they are showing the same concern for the heritage which children bring as an essential part of their humanity and responding through the curriculum.

Ultimately, of course, the issue extends beyond what is taught to the whole policy and philosophy of the school towards not only minority groups but the individuality of human beings, and beyond the school to the nation. What kind of Britain do we want?

Some questions to discuss are:

- Do we want children to grow up proud of their cultures and remaining within them?
- Is our goal assimilation or integration? (What do we mean by these concepts?)
- What, we might ask, would we want to retain if we went to live in Nepal or Tunisia? What would we expect to give up and be willing to part with?
- What do we encourage people who settle in Britain to keep? What do we ask children to surrender?

It is important to know where our children and their parents stand with regard to religion **wherever we are teaching.** This is not trespassing upon their privacy if done for the right reason. The motive is the same as wishing to know about a child's numeracy or stage of language development. We must not assume religious knowledge or affiliation or a positive attitude. If we do our teaching is likely to be ineffective and the aim of RE cannot be achieved.

Possibly because it seems to smack of prying, teachers tend not to know what the family religions of their children are even in a multifaith school.

'I think they are Muslims'
'One or two may be Hindus, but most are Sikhs, I can tell by their hair'

are the kinds of replies that one gets when questions about religious adherence are asked on INSET courses or visits to schools. (The dog is a polluting animal for Muslims, thus to bring a guide-dog into a classroom of Muslims may not be wise without warning them beforehand. This obviously cannot be done if the religious identity of the children is not known. Not all Sikhs keep uncut hair so lack of a topknot may not indicate an absence of Sikhs.)

Through names, the use of artefacts, photographs of local religious buildings on the wall, it should be possible to discover the religious background of most children after a few days.

They will soon tell you:

'That's where I go',

or Grandma does, or

'My mum uses one of those when she says her prayers.'

Young children will not know yet whether they are 'Christian' or 'Muslim' and they may not know the words 'mandir' or 'prayer carpet', but there are things with which they are familiar which indicate their identity.

Knowing where children are is important in any school and so is knowing something about the faiths from which they come. This is as true of Jehovah's Witnesses as it is of Mirpuri Muslims. Yet often one is asked: 'Why don't *they* celebrate birthdays?'

How well do we know our children? Have we ever invited a local elder of the Jehovah's Witness community into our school to explain those beliefs which it is important for us to know about and to help us respond better to their children? They care for their children as much as any parents do and are eager for them to be happy at school. Teachers have been helped greatly by such discussions.

Can Jehovah's Witnesses present a greater challenge to our ability to respect others than Jews or Muslims do?

At last we are ready to teach. We have dealt with topics and themes elsewhere (Chapter 6), here we want to emphasize that choice is important.

'How can I fit Islam into a topic on the sea?' is a question we still cannot answer. The story of Arab/Muslim exploration should have a place in history or geography but what would the RE element be? To help us we'd be looking for a different topic. If, for example, we chose 'Water' we could bring in ablutions, and the story of the Zam Zam in Islam, and the sea too with Muslim exploration and Muslims' contribution to navigation.

Topics in a multifaith school need to be chosen in such a way that no children feel that their tradition is excluded. This may appear to be a tall order but it didn't surprise us some years ago to hear of Muslims in a secondary school who appeared resentful of RE when we discovered that Islam featured only in form four and then only for a few weeks. The rest was Christianity. It is dismaying, but only to be expected, that many black youngsters are put off history because it is 'the white man's history' – Florence Nightingale but no mention of Mary Seacole – and put off religious education because it is 'about your religion, not ours', to quote one teenager. In fact such young people sometimes give as a reason for choosing sciences rather than humanities the fact that they are more culture free and so less threatening to their identity.

To involve all the cultures is important for the children who belong to them. It enhances their self-esteem. It is important for the rest. It encourages them to have respect for their peers of other traditions.

The practical solution to giving four or five cultures a place may well lie in group work. Take a topic on buildings, for example. Everyone can work on the pyramids or the local castle, but when it comes to places of worship and there may be eight which children in the class attend, no one wants to be left out. They might then be split into eight groups, each finding out about one and at the end of the period of research reporting back to the class with a presentation lasting anything up to an hour depending on the time available and success of the research.

Should membership of the groups be determined by faith, the Muslims studying the mosque? Should no one be allowed to research their own place or worship? Should one faith member be permitted to be in the group to act as leader?

These are matters to be decided in advance and the teacher's decision must finally be determined by professional judgement taking into account such concerns as socialization, group co-operation, willingness to learn from others and readiness to learn about things which are not our own in terms of parental tradition. If this were our class our aim would be to create such a comfortable relationship that we need not have all the Anglicans or Pentecostalists or Sikhs studying only their own building. Our aspiration might well be to see the mandir group asking for help from the Hindus scattered elsewhere as well as looking for information from books. Of course, in the next topic, say on festivals, the groups can be changed so that no one arrangement becomes permanent.

What of the children who belong nowhere? If groupings are not by faith the problem is reduced, but the child of no faith community is someone religious education has usually neglected. S/he should not be ignored any longer or assumed to be a Christian, a response which may be disrespectful to the child and to the religion.

Festivals

A specific section has been given to festivals as they feature prominently in primary-school life (Chapter 14). There is, however, a need to mention a few things here. In every school it would appear wise to range beyond the faith or faiths represented in it. While one wishes to endorse the faiths present it is not enough to ignore others, probably Buddhism. A real test of openness or tolerance is the ability to be concerned about or interested in *other* religions, i.e. the ones that belong to none of us.

The key question for most schools is:

'How much time can we give to Eid, Diwali, Guru Nanak's birthday, Hanukah, and Christmas?'

Teachers may say,

'You can forget trying to add Chinese New Year, we haven't any of *them* in the school! Enough is enough!'

This despairing cry is sometimes made by the very people who would encourage our traditional school to celebrate Diwali. Taken to its logical conclusion, however, it is arguing that the curriculum should be determined by the composition of the school, a mind-restricting exercise. Even in a multifaith school, where horizons may be broad, children should learn that the world extends even beyond them. A test of real openness in a class of Hindu, Muslim and Christian children may be learning about the Buddha, for example.

Is our capacity to think clearly blurred by the school Christmas, which lasts at least three weeks and has been known to be half a term long? One cheer might be made for the National Curriculum if it reduces Christmas to two weeks, at most! Pesach (Passover) is a week long but normal work is carried out on five of the days. In India Guru Nanak's birthday comes and goes in a day and even Diwali lasts only two in reality. The Eids are of the same length. For many Christians life cannot stop for more than a day, if at all, and that includes many in India.

In all schools the Christmas festivities would not suffer by being abbreviated. In multifaith schools a month on Christmas compared with a day for Guru Nanak's birthday or that of the Prophet Muhammad is more than a reflection of tradition. It is a statement of priority. The answer is to observe the major festivals of the faiths of the children in our schools, but with a sense of proportion and with sensitivity. Sikhs ask only for an assembly and perhaps a lesson to acknowledge Guru Nanak's birthday. They should certainly receive no less.

Christianity in the Multifaith School

Anyone living in Britain needs to understand Christianity in the same way that anyone living in Pakistan must understand Islam. However, tact is required in presenting Christianity and care should be given to the allocation of time and to where elements appear in the course. To begin with it in every topic may not be very smart!

To imply that Christianity is the norm is dangerously easy. 'Eid (ul Fitr) isn't like Christmas. It doesn't always fall on the same date in the year' was a statement made in a TV *Watch* programme. But it does. It is always on the first day of the month Shawwal. The commentator actually said, 'Eid isn't like *our* Christmas', thus immediately creating an 'us and them' situation and indicating an unconscious cultural bias. To make comparisons is easy and tempting. We have all done it. Let us celebrate differences instead by inviting children to enter into the mosque, Diwali, or Christian baptism without necessarily wishing to use things in their own traditions as reference points. (We might reflect for a moment on the helpfulness of being told that the Qur'an is about as long as the New Testament.)

You may like to discuss these issues.

- A teacher says, 'I can only teach what I believe.'

   (a) How would you respond if you were a headteacher to someone who expressed this view during an interview? (N.B. Interviewing panels have no right to ask candidates for posts in maintained schools questions about their religious beliefs but interviewees can disclose such information if they wish.)

   (b) How would you expect a Sikh parent to react if the teacher made this comment at a parents' evening?

   (N.B. We didn't say that the teacher was a Christian. S/he might have been a Muslim. Should that make any difference to your reaction? If so why?)

- A teacher says, 'We don't teach Islam here. If they've come to our country they must learn about our religion.' The remark is heard by a Hindu parent, who brings it to a governors' meeting. How would you advise them to handle the situation?

- A headteacher from a school in Devon says, 'We only teach Christianity in my school because we don't have any other religions in it.' Would you attach much importance to the statement in considering whether to appoint her to be head of your school?

Summary of the Position

The reasons for including religions other than Christianity in the primary school have been mentioned at various places in this book, perhaps not explicitly but where reference has been made to things like openness, respect for people, preparation for life in the actual world of today and tomorrow, preparation for life in Britain in the nineties and beyond, an understanding of beliefs and values, learning to live with differences. Much is said about depriving children of their national heritage. We would not want that, but we are very conscious that we should have been introduced to our world heritage, which we have had to discover for ourselves. We would like future generations to become aware of it in school. There is also the important point that it is very difficult to understand, examine and explore that which is one's own. We take it for granted, whatever it is, because it is so familiar. This goes for dress, food, language structure, art, and musical forms. Whatever we were brought up in is normal and often we cannot analyse it because we cannot stand back from it and get it in perspective (any more than we can relationships with our nearest and dearest)! A holiday abroad has provoked many people to look at the landscape, customs, and food of their native land for the first time. It has been said that he who knows one religion knows no religion for the same reason. Perhaps it is not until we sit through a service in a gurdwara, not understanding a word but observing what is happening, that we are provoked to think about the things we have done for years in our own place of worship if we have one, and to ask ourselves what worship is. If we want to discover how beliefs and values are formed and how they affect people it may be best not always to start at 'home' where the process was unconscious for much of our early lives. Looking at the unfamiliar may equip us with skills and the curiosity to examine things we think we know well. To be able to reflect upon, study, and criticize positively our own culture, whatever it is, would seem to be the mark of an educated person, as well as something which forces hostile to all cultures compel us to do whether we like it or not. In school we can, we hope, help children to engage in the process of open reflection in an unthreatened way.

Teaching Other World Religions

We now turn to the practical issue of how to go about it. From the first weeks in school children can be made aware of the rich variety of lifestyles, lands, people and foods which make up the world they live in. (After all they are probably introduced to elephants and giraffes before they reach school, though such animals are hard to find in the plains and hills of Britain!) Colour photographs on the classroom walls can bring home this variety to them. But try to make sure the people in them are smiling and avoid black-and-white 'Oxfam image' pictures. At storytime we can tell a story from India, Africa, Denmark, or China, it doesn't have to be religious, and back it up with some food, Indian sweets, Caribbean bananas, telling the children how, for example, if they lived in one of those islands they could pick the fruit fresh in their garden. Further back-up could be in the form of greetings, 'Namaste', and putting on a sari if our story is from India. Hopefully positive images will provided before the racism which is endemic in British society, and claims its victims by the time they are nine years old, has got to work.

The next stage is learning about some practices and related stories, and ways of life. Just as we would be taking the children to a church, inviting a minister to simulate baptism, bringing in a nun to talk about her life, looking at how Christians worship, so too we can find out about the life of a Buddhist monk, the mosque and Muslim prayers. Even if there is no mosque locally which we can visit, we can use a prayer carpet and compass to make it interesting.

The following lists indicate some areas in specific religions which might be explored in primary schools. They are not intended to be prescriptive. Ideas for activities and active learning are also provided but remember that they should be used to develop skills, attitudes and concepts, especially the latter (see Chapter 6).

Aspects of Buddhism

The Buddha, some stories of his life and, carefully dealt with, of his former lives (perhaps with older pupils where the ideas behind them can be discussed)

Some precepts, e.g. the Five Precepts which lay people as well as monks promise to keep

The Eightfold Path

Festivals

The sangha, life of a monk, nun

Temples, worship, meditation

The concept of 'change'

Active learning and activities

Drama

Collage

Visits

Visitors

Making greetings cards

Planning a journey to a Buddhist country

Creative writing about the visit

Meditating (It is important that parents are consulted about this.)

Simulations, e.g. an alms round, a puja

Role-playing stories or dramatizing them as aids to discovering their inner meanings

Aspects of Hinduism

The mandir

Puja

The Gods

Janamsanskar (birth)

Vivaha (marriage)

Antyeshti (funeral)

Family and home life

Festivals and myths associated with them

Village life

Pilgrimage

M.K. Gandhi

Hindu migration to Britain

Karma and samsara

Active learning and activities

Collage

Poems

Learning some Sanskrit/Hindi writing

Planning a journey to India

Creative writing about the visit

Dramatizing stories

Putting on a sari

Cookery

An India day

An India exhibition to be set up in the hall for parents' evening

Celebrating a festival

Making greetings cards

Games (grand)parents played in India

Making a model village

Visiting a mandir

Puja simulation

Preparing an assembly using some of the above items

Taking photos/making a video

Aspects of Islam

The Qur'an

Women and the family

Almsgiving and ethics

Ramadan and the Eids

The mosque

Prayer

The Hajj

Muhammad

Dress

The Islamic calendar

The Five Pillars

Active learning and activities

Making a prayer carpet

Learning how a prayer carpet is used

Simulating prayer

Visiting a mosque

Making a model of a mosque/the Ka'aba

Arabic writing

Learning some Arabic

Making a Qur'an stand

Tesselations and altair design

Dressing up

Cookery

Games (grand)parents played in Pakistan/Egypt/Nigeria . . .

Making Eid cards

Planning a journey to Makkah

Planning a journey to a Muslim country

Creative writing about the visit

Drama, but this must be handled with care. **No prophet or caliph should be portrayed in drama or artwork.** However, an Eid meal could be enacted with Dad or Mum telling relevant stories.

Collecting stamps with Islamic aspects

Aspects of Judaism

Pesach (Passover) and other festivals

The Jewish home and Shabbat (the Sabbath), which will include diet

The Torah

The synagogue and worship

Prayer, including the laying of tefillin

The story of Anne Frank

Some stories from the Jewish Bible and other sources

Belief in historical purpose

Active learning and activities

Hebrew writing

Learning some Hebrew

Model making, e.g. a synagogue, Torah scroll

Making a Torah pointer and a kippur/yarmulka

Learning to lay tefillin and put on a prayer shawl

Simulating a Shabbat or Pesach meal

Making matzot, latkes and other foods – a Jewish visitor might assist

Making New Year cards

Planning a journey to Israel

Creative writing about a visit to Jerusalem

Dramatizing some Jewish stories

Celebrating a festival

Visiting a synagogue

A visit from a rabbi (discuss with him or her beforehand what, if any, food he or she
    would eat or drink)

Aspects of Sikhism

Gurdwara and worship

Guru Granth Sahib

Langar

Amrit sanskar (initiation)

Sewa (community service)

Baisakhi

Five K's and turban

Birth (janam sanskar)

Weddings (anand karaj)

Death

The Punjab

Migration (including reasons for it to U.K.)

The Gurus

The oneness of God

Ethics (including sewa)

Women

Active learning and activities

Making a model gurdwara

Making a palki (canopy for Guru Granth Sahib)

Making human models to dress in Five K's and turban/wedding clothes

Visiting a gurdwara

Gurmukhi writing (Mul mantra/own names)

Learning some Punjabi, e.g. Mul mantra

Preparing karah parshad

Games (grand)parents played

Making gurpurb/mela/wedding cards

Planning a journey to the Punjab/Amritsar

Creative writing about the visit

Drama (Some Sikhs are not happy at a Guru being represented so it may be better to avoid this, but an amrit ceremony or wedding could be simulated.)

The above suggestions of content should be considered in the context of skills, concepts and attitudes mentioned on page 34. A content-laden syllabus could not in itself meet the need to facilitate the development of a child's spirituality.

Having looked through these lists and the Christianity list in Chapter 8 you might like to consider for yourself or discuss with colleagues what children should know about Christianity, Islam and other religions by the ages of seven and eleven as well as looking at guidelines which your LEA may have produced. What specifically should comprise their portrait of Jesus, Guru Nanak, or their understanding of Christmas or Muslim worship? (Don't forget to consider skills, attitudes and concepts: see Chapter 6, p. 34.)

Of course you will not be able to cover all aspects of every religion. You might discuss which ones to draw on and why.

There are three models to choose from:

1. You could decide that Christianity and one or two other religions should be studied.

2. You could draw on any tradition, using the most appropriate examples, so that in looking at scriptures in worship you might not include Hindu scriptures, since their place is not very obvious, but in examining ideas of God the Hindu contribution would be very important.

3. You could use all six major religions in relatively equal proportions while observing the caveat just made.

All three approaches can be justified educationally. Perhaps the second offers most flexibility, expecially if you have children of yet more religions, for example, Jains in Leicester, in your class.

CHAPTER
10

STORIES AND SCRIPTURES

Stories are often captivating and absorbing and can play an important part in primary education.

You may find it useful to consider the use of stories in the curriculum generally. Discuss with a colleague if possible, or consider as an individual all the purposes and benefits of telling or reading stories with pupils and write down a list. If you are discussing this with a number of colleagues, compare notes and produce a composite list before reading on.

Amongst your list(s) you will probably have included:

- communicating facts;
- challenging and provoking further thought;
- stimulating an emotional response;
- developing language;
- providing opportunities for pupils to identify with characters and reflect upon experiences without personal involvement.

Now it will be helpful to look again at the four main areas of religious education which are generally identified by LEA Agreed Syllabuses:

- awareness of self;
- relationships;
- responses to the natural world;
- understanding religious beliefs, practices and experiences.

Consider how many of these four areas (or those in your local Agreed Syllabus) can be explored through stories and are compatible with your lists of purposes and benefits.

We suspect and hope that your answers will reveal that most, if not all, are. Stories treated sensitively and, in some cases, with suitable development can provide an invaluable resource for RE in schools.

Stories can be treated in different ways in the classroom. Some are best just told and allowed to speak for themselves, but at some point in the primary age range children can be encouraged to look into stories and unravel their layers of meaning. Many stories have an obvious message, like some of Aesop's fables for example, but some are rich in allegory and metaphor and deserve closer scrutiny. Posing challenging questions such as:

'Does this story remind you of another situation?'
'Does this character remind you of anyone?'
'What does this story say to you?'
'Do you think there is a hidden message in this story?'

can encourage pupils to reflect on what they hear and start to understand that stories can embody certain messages.

Perhaps the teacher's intention in telling a certain story is to convey some idea or information to the class which requires reinforcement and development. This, then, is another opportunity for activities such as model making, collage, painting, role-play, puppet making or dance, music or poetry. Pupils will become involved in the ideas or facts and reflect on them, discuss them and perhaps develop them, or maybe just understand a little better the information which the story conveys. Teachers will need to consider carefully what they hope to achieve with the story and activities, decide how much time to invest and plan accordingly.

Having thought about the wealth of possibilities, teachers might consider, in contrast, the usefulness of a common school experience a generation or so ago when children were asked, on hearing a story, to write about it and draw a picture. The curriculum now offers a far more imaginative diet. Stories can contribute to all areas of the curriculum but we intend to highlight their benefits for religious education. If pupils are provided with the skills and inspiration to look at stories and unravel their deeper meanings, we are giving them access to understanding religious beliefs and values, which are endemic in all religious writings. Careful selection is essential, however, and stories should contribute to planned schemes of work.

Faith Stories

Looking at 'religious' stories can make a strong contribution to RE lessons. These stories may or may not be extracts from sacred literature but they are told within faith communities and can reveal something important about faith and belief. There are many tales available now produced particularly for young readers or listeners, appropriately told and well illustrated.

Creation stories from various cultures can be particularly fascinating and can help pupils understand how communities view the world, what they consider its purpose to be, and what they think about the place of humankind in the pattern of things. The Chinese tale of creation, for example, reveals belief in Yin and Yang, the two powerful, opposing forces which keep the world in peace and harmony. From their energy the Great Giant P'an Ku was created, who toiled relentlessly sculpturing the world until, exhausted, he died. Yet from his body, bones and hair the earth was clothed with rivers, forests and mountains and the parasites from his body became the first inhabitants of the earth. (This story may be found in *Exploring a Theme. The Environment*, published by CEM, or *Worlds of Difference*, by Martin Palmer and Esther Bisset, published by Blackie.)

Then there are the stories of people guided by their particular faith and beliefs – how their faith and commitment has led them to great feats of courage and achievement (Gladys Aylward, Mother Teresa or Albert Schweitzer, for example). There are also the parables, or metaphorical tales which convey, albeit not overtly, a spiritual meaning and can provide insights into religious ethics and doctrine ('The Widow's Mite' or 'The Lost Sheep' from the

Christian tradition, or the Jataka tales in Buddhism, for example). And then there are the great myths and legends of the past which express so much about humankind's feelings and beliefs, such as the ancient Hindu tales of gods and goddesses or the great stories of Roman deities.

The Bible in RE

Perhaps the most commonly told stories in RE are those found in the Bible, but teachers should consider carefully which stories they might select, and why they would be telling them. Because they are in the Bible is not sufficient reason in itself, for many Bible stories are quite inappropriate for young pupils. Consider, for example, the story of David and Bathsheba in an adulterous relationship. Would we select such a story to tell primary children if it were found on the secular shelves of a library? Similarly, Abraham's willingness to sacrifice Isaac, his son, is an alarming concept and a small child might not get to the heart of the story but might focus more on the horrific aspects.

When planning a thematic approach to religious education some teachers naturally turn to the Bible for appropriate material. The Bible does provide a rich source of material but teachers should select with caution.

Take the theme 'Water', for example, and consider which Bible stories might be selected. There are many, such as 'Jesus Turns Water into Wine', 'Jesus Walks on the Water', 'Moses in the Bullrushes', 'The Parting of the Reed Sea', 'Noah's Ark', 'Jesus Calms the Storm', 'John Baptizes Jesus', and so on. But are all these, or indeed any, appropriate for contributing to the religious dimension of the theme?

Teachers should ask the question 'What are these stories really about?' If the answer is, as in the case of Jesus turning water into wine, walking on the water or calming the storm, that these are predominantly about Jesus the miracle worker, then they do little to help pupils understand about water. These particular stories point to the divinity of Jesus and might be better placed in a theme about the life and works of Jesus or a theme about miracles with Key Stage 3 or 4 pupils who are better equipped to grapple with these sophisticated concepts. Water is in the narrative but not in the message of the story.

The same might be said of Moses in the bullrushes and the parting of the Reed Sea, which illustrate God's intervention and guiding hand throughout the history of the Jewish people and the life and influence of a great leader – Moses. These stories would have more meaning in a theme about the Jewish festival of Pesach (Passover) or great leaders.

The story of Noah's Ark is great fun with young pupils and provides plenty of opportunities for art, drama, music and language work, but this age group would focus on the animals and Noah's family, the actual flood playing a minor role. Older pupils, however, might look at the flood story, alongside the creation stories in Genesis, in order to understand the Judaeo-Christian view that water represents chaos. Noah's Ark might be saved, therefore, to contribute to a 'Water' theme with Key Stage 3 or 4 pupils.

Younger children would do better to start with their own experiences of water. They should be encouraged to understand the qualities and uses of water in their lives, and thereby begin to understand why and how it is commonly used symbolically in religious practice. Suitable Bible references are John the Baptist baptizing Jesus and stories of baptisms in the Acts of the Apostles. These stories demonstrate the symbolic use of water in Jesus' time and relate to the Christian practice of baptism today, which may well be within the experience of some of the children in the primary classroom. This can be introduced alongside examples of current uses of water in religious practice from various faith traditions. (These ideas have already been examined in more detail on pp. 29–33.)

The 'miracle' stories of Jesus turning water into wine, walking on water or calming the storm are not relevant to the theme 'Water', but when might they be suitable? Should we tell the stories we were told?

Miracles

Teachers will often say that hearing the miracle stories of Jesus, for example, did them no harm. Such teachers are usually Christians. We come across students on curriculum courses, and teachers supervising students on teaching practice, non-specialists in RE, who tell us that they were adversely affected. As they put away Father Christmas and fairy tales so they dismissed the stilling of the storm, Jesus walking on the water, the turning of water into wine, and the rest of the miracles, and were inhibited from giving religion any further serious thought. Personal experiences of someone in the family suffering caused them to doubt the healing miracles. 'Such things don't happen', they bitterly attest.

Let us take the discussion a little further. A favourite story among teachers is 'The Feeding of the Five Thousand'. The most popular form of the story is that found in the Gospel of John (6:5–13), which mentions a boy who provides the loaves and fishes. It reads:

> When Jesus looked up and saw a great crowd coming towards him, he said to Philip, 'Where shall we buy bread for these people to eat?' He asked this only to test him, for he already had in mind what he was going to do.
>
> Philip answered him, 'Eight months' wages would not buy enough bread for each one to have a bite!'
>
> Another of the disciples, Andrew, Simon Peter's brother, spoke up, 'Here is a boy with five small barley loaves and two small fish, but how far will they go among so many?'
>
> Jesus said, 'Have the people sit down.' There was plenty of grass in the place, and the men sat down, about five thousand of them. Jesus then took the loaves, gave thanks, and distributed to those who were seated as much as they wanted. He did the same with the fish.
>
> When all had had enough to eat, he said to his disciples, 'Gather the pieces that are left over. Let nothing be wasted.' So they gathered them and filled twelve baskets with the pieces of the five barley loaves left over by those who had eaten.

Similar accounts are also found in the other gospels.

Before we think about what children make of this story, you might like to write down your own thoughts. What is its message?

If you have told primary-school children this or any miracle story what kinds of questions did they immediately ask? None at all? Isn't that strange when they are usually filled with questioning curiosity? Why didn't they show their normal inquisitiveness? Is it that they have been encouraged to think that religion is unlike any other sphere of knowledge or aspect of education – one to be accepted uncritically? A strange notion! Not one shared by Jesus, Guru Nanak, the Prophet Muhammad, or the Buddha, to name only a few. Their messages depended for success on audiences which were willing to challenge the conventions which they questioned.

If children did talk about the story they probably asked how it happened. Immediately we have an apparent difficulty. We don't know. We weren't there. The choice seems to lie between:

- making a statement which discloses our belief, e.g. 'It happened as the story says it did', or 'Jesus was God's son, he could do anything';
- requiring uncritical acceptance of the biblical account, saying, in effect, 'That is what the Bible says, take it or leave it';
- trying to rationalize it by saying such things as, 'The little boy probably shamed the others into giving up their food'. But read 'The Feeding of the Four Thousand', where the Gospel of Mark (8:2) states 'they had nothing to eat'. All the other versions imply this, including the one in John.

Actually the story has nothing to do with caring and sharing but is concerned with proclaiming that Jesus is the Messiah, as can be seen when the whole of John 6 is read. At the end the people want to make Jesus their king.

Of a similar kind are rationalizations in terms of what we adults call psychosomatic medicine, as explanations of the healing miracles. All these approaches miss the point that the miracles are affirmations of the divinity of Jesus or other aspects of theology. As such they are devalued when they are presented to young children who cannot understand the theology and must necessarily concentrate on what are actually irrelevant matters. The miracles are concerned with who Jesus is and where his authority comes from, not with *how* he did things. Older children should certainly grapple with these issues, that is with the theology, but perhaps not until Key Stage 3 or 4.

The Parables

The parables seem to provide more useful material for discussion with children, though of course their experiences and therefore perspectives will not be those of an adult. The well-known response of the seven-year-old girl to the story of the Prodigal Son (Luke 15:11–32) – 'I don't think much of that daddy. My daddy wouldn't have let me go by myself' – is indicative of the way in which children home in on things which matter to them and which they can make sense of and ignore the rest. Jesus told parables like this one to provoke his audience to think and respond. The Bible doesn't always say what the answer should be so that Christians can still find some parables very puzzling today. Teachers might restrain themselves from telling children 'You're wrong' and, instead, allow them to think for themselves, as Jesus did. Thinking, however, can be based only on previous knowledge and, especially, experience. That is why Jesus grounded the parables in everyday life. There is no sense in introducing parables prematurely.

Re-expressing a parable does not seem to be a good idea. When Christianity became a gentile religion in the Roman Empire the Good Samaritan did not become the Kind Barbarian and a modern race-relations slant wouldn't necessarily be helpful or faithful to the original. The choice would seem to be:

- not to use it;
- to miss out the detail and minimally edit the story;
- to wait till the later years of Key Stage 3 when the necessary background can be provided. There is an element of Palestinian history and geography which children must know if they are to understand the life and ministry of Jesus, but it should be kept to a minimum and studied only to make the gospel material intelligible.

Could you provide a form of the story of the Good Samaritan, for your use, which is faithful to the text as far as it goes, so that a later teacher can supplement what you have done rather than having to undo it? Would it be permissible simply to say that Jesus once told a story about a man who was beaten up and robbed; rather than help some men passed him by, and it was left to a foreigner to carry him to safety? Perhaps we should ask ourselves why we want to use the parable at all. If it is to encourage neighbourliness that is more likely to be done through developing relationships in the classroom and the school than by telling stories with a moral. Virtues are acquired by practice and in the company of the virtuous, not by listening to moral precepts. If sermons are often lost on believing and consenting adults how much less effective are they likely to be with children? Perhaps the parables are better left until the decisive, challenging element which most of them contain can be examined. Otherwise they are likely to be neutralized, reduced to the level of narrative, which is unjust to Jesus, the evangelists, and Christianity.

After this brief excursion into theology, unavoidable if we are teaching about religions, we can return to the classroom. A common and understandable response to suggestions that the miracles and parables of Jesus should be treated with caution in the primary school is an anxious:

'What *can* we teach then?'

In other words, what criteria can we use to help us select suitable biblical material?

A good starting-point might be the criteria applied to *any* stories selected for young pupils. Choosing the right stories for children is a talent teachers acquire which becomes almost instinctive, but stop for a moment and consider why some stories are appropriate and others not.

Imagine that a student teacher, on teaching practice with your class, asks you for guidelines for selecting suitable stories for telling primary pupils. You might like to produce a list of questions for the student to ask him/herself about a story. Compare notes with a colleague if possible.

The same questions can be asked of biblical material. If the pupils might not understand a story, then it is best left until they are older; if the story might cause fear or distress, then naturally it will be rejected. Should the biblical material be so complex that confusion and misconceptions may arise, or should it not make the point intended, or should it not relate to anything the pupils already know and understand, then it must be considered inappropriate and more suitable material might be found elsewhere. The Bible can provide pupils with a greater understanding of Christianity and aspects of Judaism, but the material must be selected carefully to suit the abilities of the pupils and to fit into an overall framework of RE. Otherwise a Bible story is not religious education, it is merely a story for story's sake.

An example of a story pupils might be encouraged to explore is the calling of the fishermen disciples, described in a few sentences in the Gospel of Mark (1:16–20). Behind the challenge is the question of what was going on in the mind of Jesus and the men he summoned.

The story as it stands suggests that Jesus had second sight and that the fishermen responded to a call that they could not possibly understand, to become 'fishers of men'. What lies behind the narrative? Were they already friends? Had Jesus discussed his mission with them already? Were they told to continue with their normal jobs until this moment came? The teacher might reflect on this. Children might begin by thinking about such things as what kind of person they would choose to take with them on holiday or on a picnic or to play in a team game. Then they might be able to move on to what kinds of people Jesus wanted, why he chose men and not women, why he chose some fishermen, why they were prepared to join him and what kind of man he was. This kind of approach makes the story real for young pupils.

Consider, also, the importance of putting a story into context. The Easter story, for example, may have little meaning to pupils from non-Christian homes, but if it is told as one which is remembered in churches during the festival of Easter, and explained with the help of Easter gardens, or the Christian symbols of Jesus on the cross or the empty cross, then pupils will be better able to realize the significance of the story to Christians.

Given careful treatment a simple Bible story might take on the depth of meaning that it had when first told to new Christians or when it actually happened. Stories live and become meaningful as they capture the imagination.

Scriptures

All the major world faiths have sacred writings which express some of the beliefs and values of faith communities. This material, however, is not always easily accessible to pupils in primary schools. English translations of the Qur'an (Muslim), the Guru Granth Sahib (Sikh) or the many Hindu and Buddhist scriptures tend to be found in the realms of higher or adult education and in language not always suitable for primary-school readership. This should not, however, preclude investigating sacred writings of various faiths within primary RE schemes of work. There are many stories about Hindu Gods and Goddesses retold in English from the Hindu scriptures suitable for primary- and middle-school children, as there are Buddhist tales. There is little story content in the Qur'an or the Guru Granth Sahib, but tales told within the faith communities would provide useful material in schools and are readily available. Some suitable books are suggested in the Resources section (p. 98).

But investigating the contents is only one dimension. Looking at the history of, the particular rituals associated with and the attitudes towards sacred writings can make a valuable contribution to pupils' religious understanding. Towards the upper end of the primary age range pupils will have some understanding of time scale, and it is at this stage that they can investigate how some sacred writings, including the Bible, came to be written, by whom and for what purpose.

Younger pupils will be interested to know how various books are treated by their faith communities and can enjoy role-play, art, craft and design activities. Role-playing the Simhat Torah celebration in Judaism, for example, can help pupils understand how Jewish people value, celebrate and give thanks for the gift of the Torah. They could make Torah scrolls, design covers, and parade the scrolls around the classroom, singing and waving flags.

Or perhaps pupils could make a shoe-box palki (canopy) and a small model of a granthi reading the Guru Granth Sahib in its prestigious place within the gurdwara. Children could begin to see the importance of the Guru Granth and how the book is seen by the Sikh community as their Guru, or teacher, now and for the future.

Fictional Tales

A chapter on stories would not be complete without mentioning fictional tales. These are particularly useful for developing the implicit dimension of RE, the area concerned with the child's personal feelings and responses in life, although some fictional tales can introduce explicit material also. Fictional stories can raise important questions, engage the child's imagination and develop a sense of mystery and awe – such important areas for contributing to a child's spiritual development.

Fictional stories can enable pupils to identify with characters and vicariously enter into their situations and adventures. Through them children can find an expression of personal fears, griefs, hopes and aspirations which they may be unable to articulate. Having addressed these issues through listening, reading and becoming involved in the plot, they may be better equipped, not only to deal with situations life will present to them, but to relate to and sympathize with the feelings and behaviour of others. Here is an essential element of religious education.

CHAPTER
11

ACTIVE LEARNING IN RELIGIOUS EDUCATION

Teachers have been aware for many years that pupils learn more readily by 'doing' and this is particularly well illustrated in modern maths and science classes, where pupils hypothesize, manipulate and experiment as part of the learning process.

If children are actively participating and involved in the learning process, rather than passively listening, then there are several benefits. One, most obvious, is that pupils appear to enjoy their lessons more, and they are generally better motivated. They have ownership of the task in hand, which enhances a sense of achievement and often pride. Many of a child's senses can be involved in the active learning process and, perhaps as a result of this alongside higher motivation, pupils often appear to understand and thereby retain the information more readily.

Teachers, too, may share in the learning process and discover pupils' understanding and interpretations of information as they explore together. Active learning has now become an integral part of the assessment programme in many schools and teachers are able to observe how pupils handle data, information and equipment and assess their skills and understanding.

Active learning techniques might be adopted for all areas of the curriculum, and religious education is no exception. Indeed, so much of a young child's leisure time is spent 'pretending' or 'making' it would seem wise to exploit this natural interest and direct it towards RE and the school curriculum in general.

As this book aims to involve you, the reader, in active participation, we suggest the following exercise, which might prove more beneficial if several people take part.

1. Individually make a list of all the possible active learning techniques in all areas of the curriculum (e.g. singing, cookery).

2. Compare your list with that of a colleague and compile a composite list.

3. Consider in pairs or threes which techniques would be suitable for teaching religious education.

4. You will probably have decided that most active learning techniques *are* suitable for religious education. If any caused hesitation, spend a few moments considering why.

There may be limited facilities within school so that cookery or drama, for example, may cause quite an upheaval. Perhaps links between religious-education material and activities don't easily come to mind. If this is the case, the next step in this exercise may help. If you are worried about causing offence, there are guidelines on avoiding problems later in this chapter (pp. 68–70).

5. With colleagues, suggest two or three religious themes which might be usefully explored through the active learning strategies you have listed. You will need half an hour or so to complete this task. You may like to use the following examples and (non-exhaustive) list of active learning techniques to help you.

N.B. The purpose of this exercise is to illustrate how active learning can contribute to RE and the wide range of active learning strategies at teachers' disposal. It is *not* a model for curriculum planning, where themes should be chosen then active learning strategies selected as appropriate to meet attainment targets.

Examples of Active Learning in RE

	Activity	Theme
Craft	Make a model mosque Produce a class mobile using Easter symbols	Special Places Signs and Symbols Easter
Role-play	Act out the rituals for the Jewish Friday-evening meal to welcome Shabbat (the Sabbath)	Celebration
	Ask a vicar to role-play a baptism with a doll in church	Water
Cookery	Make barfi (Indian sweets) for Diwali Make bread for Harvest Festival	Festivals of Light Harvest

To meet the demands of these tasks pupils would need to research, enquire, discuss and plan, and thereby become fully involved in the learning process. Older pupils engaged in making a model mosque, for example, might investigate a variety of pictures and slides, discover the requirements for washing facilities, for men and women to sit separately, for somewhere for children and adults to study, any signs and symbols which might be utilized and so on. They could discuss, plan, choose suitable materials and then make the final product. Younger pupils would be engaged in a simpler task such as making barfi, directed by a parent or teacher, but enjoying the active involvement, knowing that the sweets were being prepared for a special celebration.

Active Learning Techniques

Visitors

Visits

Simulation

Artefacts – discussing, handling, drawing, etc.

Poetry – writing, discussing

Videos – making them

Slides, photographs – taking them or discussing them

Pictures – discussing and analysing

Drama

Brainstorming

Discussing

Information gathering

Collages, friezes, mobiles, etc.

Displays

Devising rituals

Making models – buildings, puppets, shrines, etc.

Making greetings cards

Cookery

Dressing costume dolls

Designing and making costumes

Making music

Creating a dance

●

●

●

Plus any ideas of your own

Avoiding Problems

Religion is a sensitive, emotive subject and it is the responsibility of every teacher of religious education to encourage pupils' respect for religious beliefs and to avoid offending adherents of any faith. With this in mind, teachers must tread a careful path. Parents, too, may become anxious about children's participation in some classroom activities.

'Our teacher taught us how to pray at a Hindu shrine today.'

A comment like this from a young child may well cause alarm among parents – Hindu and non-Hindu. So teachers may well ask:

'At what point does role-play of Muslim prayer postures or puja at a Hindu shrine actually become worship?'

'To what extent can a child participate in the celebration of a festival of another faith?'

'Could making artefacts and handling sacred objects offend a faith community?'

Here we have some useful questions which can be used for active learning among staff, or parents and governors. Perhaps they could be addressed at a staff meeting when devising a school policy for RE. In the case of students or INSET, a simulation staff meeting could be devised, with each participant playing a different role – the headteacher, an enthusiastic staff member, a disenchanted teacher, a concerned parent or governor, the local vicar or leader of a faith community. The discussion might touch on the following points.

1. The Requirements of the Agreed Syllabus

First and foremost, it should be made clear to teachers, governors, parents and the pupils themselves that religious education in 'Maintained' schools (State schools) and Church Voluntary Controlled Schools must follow the guidelines of the local Agreed Syllabus for RE. Local education authorities' Agreed Syllabuses generally state that pupils should encounter and understand about religious beliefs and practices, but inculcating any particular religious beliefs is the role of the parents and the faith community to which they belong.

2. Simulation in the Classroom

Should a teacher wish pupils to begin to understand about the rituals of Hindu worship, then a most effective way might be to involve pupils in producing a shrine in the corner of the classroom. Children might paint pictures of Hindu deities, or make clay or plasticine models. They could pick flowers for an offering or make some from tissue paper. The shrine could be decorated with tinsel, paper chains and symbols, and candles could be lit (by an adult!). Children would be encouraged to consider these rituals in terms of welcoming Hindu gods.

At some point the teacher might ask a Hindu member of the class to talk about or demonstrate the puja (worship) rituals, having first elicited his/her willingness and ability to do so, or the teacher might demonstrate some of these. Some members of the class might like to role-play a Hindu family at worship – but at no stage should a teacher say that the class will pray at the shrine.

Role-playing certain aspects of puja will enable pupils to stand in the shoes of a Hindu believer and encourage respect and some understanding of Hindu worship, but the enquiring, investigative atmosphere of the classroom is not conducive to worship so participation at this level is not possible. Worship requires willingness and intention from the participants, so teachers may feel reassured that their role-play activities do not step over the line between simulation and the actual event. Children are not worshipping unless they come to the lesson with that intention. Clearly, any attempt to worship in this situation would offend both Hindus and non-Hindus alike.

3. Celebrating Festivals

In a similar way pupils can share in the celebration of festivals of various faiths. The teacher would be aiming to help pupils to understand the significance of the festival to the faith community and to get to the heart of the purpose of the celebrations. In a multifaith school all pupils might enjoy the preparations for Christmas, decorating the classroom, hearing the Nativity stories and participating in the fun of the Christmas party. When the Muslim festival of Eid ul Fitr arrives, again classmates may share in the preparations, the decorating and the feasting. The sharing of celebrations not only strengthens bonds and develops relationships, but gives pupils the opportunity to develop a real understanding about the stories, rituals and symbols associated with various festivals. It lays the foundations for greater insight into the festivals, and more important, understanding of the meanings which lie behind them. (See Chapter 14 for further details on festivals.)

In no way are pupils expected to become part of the faith community to which a festival belongs, but all pupils and staff can be enriched by sharing and enjoying the celebrations.

4. Religious Artefacts

Some teachers may be concerned about handling religious artefacts or making artefacts in a primary classroom, for fear that this may offend members of some faith communities. They are right to be cautious, but need not feel discouraged. Handling religious artefacts does demand respect, which is a valuable lesson in itself, and can bring colour and inspiration to religious education in school. This area is explored in greater detail in Chapter 13, where teachers can also find lists of artefacts suitable for classroom use.

Technology, art and craft activities (designing, drawing and making) can bring an exciting dimension to RE and lead children to further enquiries and greater understanding of religious objects and their purposes. Here are some ideas.

- Design a Muslim prayer mat.
- Make a Seder plate for Pesach (Passover).
- Produce a class collage showing the canopy over the Guru Granth Sahib in a (Sikh) gurdwara.
- Make a clay model of the Buddha.
- Produce a small Hindu shrine in a shoe-box.
- Make a chalice and patten out of yogurt pots, cardboard plates and silver foil.

If a teacher feels worried that an activity may offend, then a telephone call to a leader of the faith community for clarification is always possible and will be appreciated.

It is also wise to inform parents about the active learning strategies the school encourages as part of its religious-education programme. A clear statement of aims, intentions and some examples of practice within the school policy statement should avoid any misunderstandings and misinterpretations!

CHAPTER
12

USING CHILDREN AND OTHER FAITH MEMBERS AS RESOURCES

It is a great and natural temptation to use the Hindu or Christian child as a resource. Religion has to do with human beings and like many other things in the primary school it is most successful when it is humanized. So believers in the classroom present us with a wonderful opportunity to bring religion to life.

But let's pause for a moment to think of some occasion when we were picked on in class.

'Mary's dad's a newsagent. She can tell us how many different dailies there are.'

'Michael's mum's a dentist. He can tell us how many teeth an adult should have.'

In matters religious we are likely to ask a Hindu child how many Gods he can name although those readers who are Christians know how they would shudder and run if someone stopped them on the way out of church and asked them to explain why it was necessary for God to become incarnate! And they are articulate teachers.

Not only might the child's knowledge be slight and/or misleading, their beliefs and practices may be something they wish to keep private. A vicar's daughter became so annoyed at this disturbance to her privacy that she decided to declare herself an atheist, but that didn't help much. She was now asked for an atheist view!

We must also remember that the difference between being a believer and being a teacher or student is that the believer is doing things which are so much part of his or her life that they do not need explanation. The person who is accustomed to kneel when praying probably does not reflect on the reason for doing so until they find out that Jews stand to pray in a synagogue or, perhaps, they go to a church where the congregation sits to sing hymns and stands for prayer, as in Germany, for example. Most children do what they do because that is how they are being brought up. They cannot be expected to provide us with any better explanations for their actions than that.

Children may be used as resources so long as we have quietly, in private, discovered their willingness and negotiated the extent of their participation.

'We're going to the church that I think you go to, Robert, the one in Manvers Street, to look at the place where people get baptized. Would you like to tell us about it when we get there?'

gives Robert a chance to opt in or out and the question is put in language he can understand. 'Baptistry' and probably 'Baptist' are words which may not yet be part of his vocabulary. He may decide against involvement but start to chip in when he feels secure in the church he attends.

'That's where I sit with my mum and dad,'

he might say. Let him feel comfortable and contribute what he can and will.

Regional names for Hindu Gods, rather than the ones we find in books, 'Father Bill' instead of 'priest' or 'vicar', 'namaaz' for 'prayer', or 'babaji' instead of 'Guru Granth Sahib', all these can be reasons for children keeping silent. They don't know what we are talking about. We must try to operate at their level of religious practice. And it is the practices that they may be best able to help us with, especially if they are of primary age. Their religion is something they do. Later, and many secondary teachers can tell us how true this is, the Muslim teenager may be able to speak very articulately about Islamic beliefs.

It is also natural for children to boast. Your Sikh boy may be able to tie his own turban. Strictly speaking it should be worn only when he can do so, but many wear ready-tied ones before they have acquired this skill, to be like Dad or a pal. They may tell you they can tie it if asked. It might be wise to follow up your question with,

'Would you like to show me?'

Then, if he can,

'Would you like to show the class how you do it, when we are talking about special clothes tomorrow?'

Children come from homes that can be rich in resources of all kinds, miners' lamps, war medals, Victorian christening robes, and family Bibles as well as prayer carpets, pictures of the Taj Mahal, a mum who has been on the Hajj, a dad who can wind a turban, and one who can lay tefillin. Once interest has been aroused and confidence won the human resources and artefacts of a community can be at your disposal, but it must never be forgotten that you are the professional teacher. Faith representatives, be they children, Anglican priests or rabbis, are resources.

Perhaps the paramount reason for involving the children, their parents, and the community in what we do is one already mentioned. That is self-esteem. Teachers are often tempted to lose their professional self-respect because society does not appear to value them. They are consequently in a better position than most to appreciate the needs of others for self-respect. The child whose culture is demonstrated to be of value because it is taught about in the school, the imam or vicar whose standing in the community is given added esteem by being welcomed into the school is likely to be enriched by the experience. At the merely practical level many teachers can speak of the improvement in academic attainment in all subjects and in discipline that has resulted from such cultural recognition, and of positive developments in relationships with the community.

CHAPTER
13

USING RELIGIOUS ARTEFACTS

What is a religious artefact? You might like to give this question some thought then formulate a definition. Compare this with a definition by a colleague, or several, and discuss together suitable wording for a final statement before reading further.

You may already see from your discussions and definitions that artefacts have an important role to play in many religious practices. A religious artefact can be an object used or worn every day or only on special occasions. When used as an aid to religious rituals, particularly worship, many objects can respresent something spiritual or divine and they can provide believers with a channel to the numinous. Feelings and beliefs are projected through them and in the process, in the eyes of believers, they can become sacred and holy in themselves. For pupils to understand this particular quality is essential and religious artefacts, therefore, should be stored, displayed and handled with the utmost respect.

It is, perhaps, because of this that some teachers feel wary of introducing artefacts into the classroom for fear of misrepresenting a faith or insulting a faith community. Some artefacts would, indeed, be too sacred to handle in the classroom. The Guru Granth Sahib (the Sikh holy book), for example, which is placed on a dais under a canopy in the gurdwara (the Sikh place of worship) and ritually 'laid to rest' each evening, could not be handed around the class. Small copies of some hymns are available, however, which would enable pupils to see Punjabi writing (Gurmukhi), and posters, slides, videos and books, or even a visit to a gurdwara would show pupils the rituals involved, which illustrate how important the Guru Granth Sahib is to Sikhs.

Similarly, a non-Muslim handling the Qur'an (the holy book of Islam) may cause offence to Muslims, for the Qur'an in Arabic is viewed as the word of God. English translations are available, however, which are not seen as the true Qur'an, and a teacher could demonstrate how the Qur'an is treated with reverence by first washing his/her hands before unwrapping the book (usually wrapped for protection) and placing it on a Qur'an stand to be read. The Qur'an should never be placed under or below the level of other books, so when the teacher has completed the demonstration it should be placed carefully on a table or high shelf wrapped once more in fabric.

Muslim children in the class may well wonder what all the fuss is about and exclaim that their copies of the Qur'an are flung on the bookshelves with all the other books at home. This may well be true and illustrates for pupils the great diversity of belief and practice within any faith community. But whilst acknowledging that not all members of a particular faith necessarily demonstrate such respect, teachers should take the line which shows the utmost reverence and which is unlikely to cause offence.

If you are in doubt about any item, a telephone call to the official in the appropriate faith community will clarify the situation.

Artefacts clearly play an important role in religious practice, so introducing them in school can provide children with stimulating 'ways in' to understanding religious phenomena or can enrich and reinforce their understanding of religious rituals and beliefs. Here are some suggestions for using religious objects in the classroom.

Promoting Thought through Questions

Pupils may well be used to handling artefacts in the classroom for other areas of the curriculum. If not, perhaps a class could be introduced to some non-religious artefacts initially, such as a musical instrument or a historical object, then move on to religious items. The pupils should be encouraged to develop their skills in observing and describing objects and to build up appropriate language and articulate their ideas. Teachers can promote thinking by asking questions. Some of those below would be suitable to ask of any object, but some are more appropriate for religious artefacts. Pupils may try to answer individually or discuss in groups.

- What do you think this is?
- How do you think this is used?
- When do you think it might be used?
- Where do you think it is used?
- Who do you think uses it?
- What do you think it might signify or represent to the user?

This last question is, of course, the most important for RE, the user then being an adherent of a religious faith. The main purpose of using religious artefacts in school is to help pupils to understand their significance to the faith community.

Some pupils may have some knowledge about the object selected, or it may be totally unknown to everyone, but the exercise of considering possible uses will require them to think in terms of religious rituals and practices and actively involve them in speculation, given the evidence they have. The activity is fun and educationally worthwhile.

As pupils speculate, teachers may wish to point out certain characteristics, then ultimately reveal answers to all the questions, highlighting, as most important, the last.

Artefacts May Tell a Story

Very often an artefact provides an opening for telling a related story which can illustrate the article's importance to believers. A small Buddha rupa (statue), for example, can lead into a story of Prince Siddhartha and his path to enlightenment. A crucifix can be introduced in the spring term and can encourage older pupils to explore the Good Friday and Easter story. A

Hanukiyah, the candlestick used at the Jewish festival of Hanukah, can provide a basis for telling the story of the purification of the Temple in Jerusalem, and the lamp which burned for eight days. Stories are invaluable, but pupils might then move on to activities.

Demonstrating Religious Artefacts

Having religious artefacts in the classroom allows pupils not only to see the items, but to touch, handle, feel and smell them. Involving many senses has obvious benefits for the learner, and the inquisitive nature of many children might lead them naturally into experimentation and role-play:

- If pupils see the saffron robe of a Buddhist monk or nun, they will want to try it on and may re-enact an alms round or try some simple meditation.
- A child seeing a Muslim prayer carpet and compass will be keen to know how to find the direction of Makkah and where to place the carpet. Some Muslim pupils may point out the intricate patterns or demonstrate some prayer postures to their classmates.
- A teacher may invite a vicar to the classroom to role-play an infant baptism with a doll with young pupils after they have been introduced to a baptism candle and some cards.

The possibilities are endless and the use of artefacts can bring real liveliness to a religious-education programme.

Providing Starting-points

Once an artefact has opened a door on an area of interest, then further, related avenues can be explored. This brainstorming exercise should illustrate the point.

1. Select a familiar religious artefact – a cross, a Pascal candle or perhaps a Buddha rupa or a Jewish Seder plate – and write its name on a large sheet of paper.

2. Individually or with a colleague, write down some activities, events and information relating to your artefact to explore with pupils.

3. Now write down any avenues which could be pursued further. You might find that there are several possibilities. Links with other areas of the curriculum become apparent at this stage. You may see opportunities for language, drama, history, art and craft, technology and so on.

The diagram overleaf illustrates how a kirpan (a Sikh sword) can be used as a starting-point.

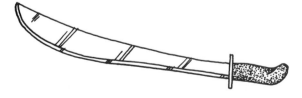

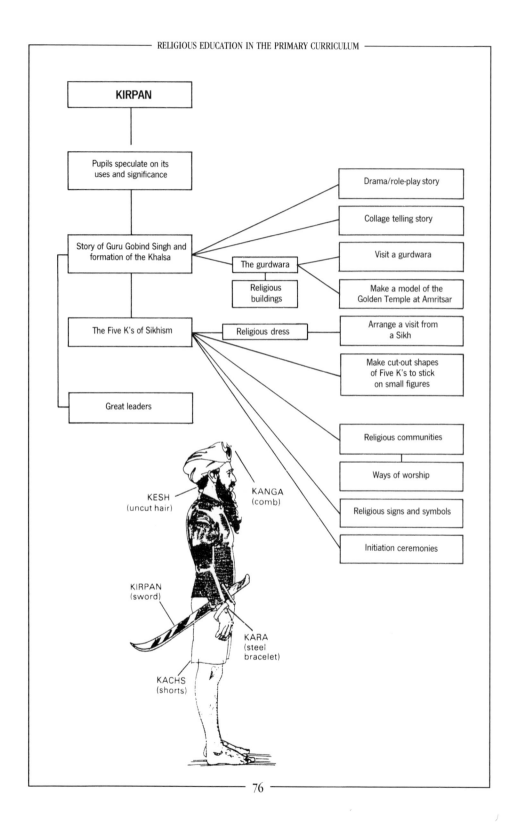

KIRPAN

Pupils speculate on its uses and significance

Story of Guru Gobind Singh and formation of the Khalsa

The gurdwara

Religious buildings

The Five K's of Sikhism

Religious dress

Great leaders

Drama/role-play story

Collage telling story

Visit a gurdwara

Make a model of the Golden Temple at Amritsar

Arrange a visit from a Sikh

Make cut-out shapes of Five K's to stick on small figures

Religious communities

Ways of worship

Religious signs and symbols

Initiation ceremonies

KESH (uncut hair)

KANGA (comb)

KIRPAN (sword)

KARA (steel bracelet)

KACHS (shorts)

Allaying Fears

Many teachers may feel wary about religious artefacts. The following exercises should help to raise the issues, give opportunities for expressing apprehensions and allay fears.

- Organize a debate with colleagues and discuss the proposal:

    'Religious artefacts are sacred objects. It is an abuse to utilize them in RE lessons in school.'

- Imagine yourself preparing to speak for both sides in the above debate and make lists of points you would like to make in support of the motion and against it.

- Role-play a discussion between a headteacher who supports his/her RE co-ordinator in the use of religious artefacts in the classroom, the RE co-ordinator, and a leader of a local religious community who complains that the objects are being misused.

- Prepare a statement to be included in the school policy booklet explaining the purpose and uses of religious artefacts in school.

Artefact Boxes

If you feel convinced that religious artefacts can make a valuable contribution to RE lessons, you may be wondering where you can find some. The best person to ask is your local RE adviser or inspector. There may well be a supply of religious artefacts available on loan to local schools. Alternatively, a college of higher education or university with a religious-studies department may have artefacts which you can borrow.

Many schools like to start their own collections or team up with other schools and share boxes. If you feel inspired, the following suggestions for boxes of artefacts and related resources may be helpful. We have also included in the Resources section (p. 100) addresses from which some of these items may be obtained.

Christening or Baptism Box

- Christening gown
- Photographs of christenings
- Christening cards
- Christening cake decorations
- Prayer-book or special printed service sheet
- Christening candle
- Pictures of fonts/baptismal tanks
- Books/posters about birth ceremonies (usually found under 'rites of passage'; see for comparison Sikh baby-naming ceremony, Jewish and Muslim birth ceremonies)

Christmas Box

- Christmas cards: wide variety showing a variety of biblical scenes and also secular cards
- Advent calendar
- Tree decorations
- Christmas cake decorations
- Pictures of Christmas food
- Small box, gift wrapped
- Pictures of Santa Claus/St Nicholas
- Christingle (orange, red ribbon, nuts and fruit, candle)
- St Lucia head garland
- Book of carols/Christmas songs
- Books/posters about Christmas traditions around the world
- Books about the birth of Jesus

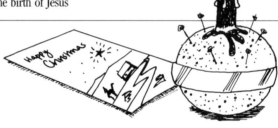

Easter Box

- Easter cards
- Pictures of Easter food
- Recipes for simnel cake/Easter biscuits
- Papier mâché hollow Easter eggs
- Chicks/bunnies
- Easter cake decorations
- Instructions for decorating Easter eggs
- Instructions for making an Easter garden
- Cross/crucifix
- Spring flowers (fabric)
- Easter candle
- Books/posters about Easter celebrations/stories

Signs and Symbols Box

- Highway Code
- Cub/brownie/scout/guide badges or hats
- Pictures of uniforms
- Books/posters showing Christian signs and symbols
- Cross
- Fish badge
- Chalice, patten and wafers
- The Five K's of Sikhism (pictures of the sword and shorts would keep the cost down): kara (bracelet), kangha (comb), kirpan (sword), kacha (shorts), kesh (uncut hair, which requires another picture); see *Baisakhi* (Living Festivals series, RMEP)
- Poster showing Muslim prayer ritual (salat)

N.B. The possibilities for this box are endless!

'Welcome Shabbat' Jewish Meal Box

- Posters/pictures about Shabbat (Sabbath)
- 2 candles and holders
- Wine bottle
- Flowers (fabric) and vase
- Yarmulkah (skull-cap)
- Kiddush cup
- Book about Shabbat (see Living Festivals series, RMEP)

N.B. When you want to use this box you will also need:

- Challah (2 plaited loaves of bread)
- Tablecloth, cutlery and glasses

Muslim Box

- Pictures of mosques
- Skull-cap
- Prayer beads (tasbih)
- Compass (qiblah)
- Examples of Muslim calligraphy patterns
- Poster of Muslim prayer ritual (salat)
- Poster of Muslim washing ritual (wuzu)
- Eid cards
- Books/posters about Islam or Muslims
- Books/posters/slides about the Hajj (pilgrimage to Makkah)

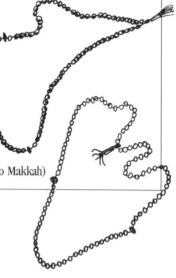

Hindu Puja Box (Articles for Worship)

- Poster of a Hindu god (Krishna is popular)
- Small brass or plaster statue of a Hindu god (Ganesha, Siva, Krishna or Laksmi)
- Joss sticks and holder
- Small metal tray (stainless steel or brass) for food offerings
- Small Indian vase for offerings of flowers
- Brass bell
- Arti lamp or nightlight
- Flowers (fabric)
- Books about Hinduism or puja
- Posters about Hindu puja

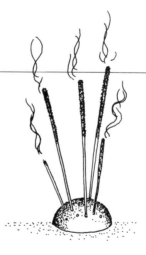

CHAPTER
14

FESTIVALS

It is in the nature of humankind to mark significant events with rituals and celebrations, so throughout history and in all cultures, there stand festivals. They offer communities a time to reflect on memorable events in their pasts, to celebrate their values and to reaffirm their common beliefs. As people celebrate through story-telling, dancing, singing, eating, giving and sharing, so bonds are strengthened and renewed within the community.

Not all festivals are joyous occasions (Ash Wednesday or the Night of Power during Ramadan, for example). Some may be serious affairs during which members of the community commemorate an important event with solemn prayers, reading and contemplation. Again important values are reaffirmed and community bonds are deepened.

Some festivals are secular (Guy Fawkes Night or American Independence, for example) whereas others have particular religious significance (such as Easter, Pesach or Wesach). Others have their roots in religious tradition but have become increasingly secularized in recent times, so that for many the festival has very little religious significance at all (Christmas for some people, and Chinese New Year, for example). Throughout each term teachers will find opportunities to explore secular and religious festivals using both familiar and less familiar examples. It may be helpful for a member of staff, possibly the RE co-ordinator, to provide a digest on festivals as a reference for their colleagues.

With some colleagues, if possible, brainstorm a particular festival on a large sheet of paper, contributing all the elements you consider are important for understanding it.

You have probably noticed from your explorations that festivals have much to offer many areas of the curriculum. Art and craft activities, technology, language work, history, geography, drama, music can all make their contribution. Festivals can be colourful and exciting and teachers might easily be seduced into investigating and participating in the 'festivities' while other important aspects remain unexplored. This model, however, illustrates how festivals can be developed for RE particularly:

The diagram classifies festivals into three main areas, story, celebration and symbol, yet there are overlaps between all three. Investigating these areas should help pupils to begin to understand *what* people remember at festivals, *when* and *how* they celebrate. To get to the heart of religious understanding, however, pupils should begin to understand *why* festivals are celebrated and what the stories, celebrations and symbols convey, at a spiritual level, to the faith community – the *inner meaning*.

The model can be applied to any festival, and should enable you to select a balance of material from all three dimensions (traditionally there has been rather more emphasis on the story dimension). You might see how the areas interrelate and ensure that your pupils are led through their investigations and activities to encounter the inner meaning.

The boxes below provide examples of frameworks from which teachers can develop lessons, activities and events appropriate to the different age ranges in school.

Ramadan and Eid ul Fitr (Islamic festival)

Inner Meaning
Service and submission to Allah; keeping one of the Five Pillars of Islam (sawm – fasting); celebration of completion of fasting; reaffirming faith and strengthening community bonds.

Story
Night of Power.

Symbol
Islamic patterns; Arabic calligraphy.

Celebration
Fasting; feasting; special foods; exchanging gifts and cards; wearing new clothes; family gatherings.

Diwali (Hindu festival)

Inner Meaning

Good triumphs over evil; new beginnings and hopes for prosperity in the new year.

Story

Ramayana; Laksmi.

Symbol

Rangoli patterns; diva lamps; fireworks; images of deities (Rama, Sita, Hanuman, Laksmi).

Celebration

Dramas and puppet plays, dance, music and songs; spring cleaning; decorations; diva lamps; special food; family gatherings; exchange of gifts and cards.

Easter

Inner Meaning

Darkness/light; death/new life; sadness/joy; reconciliation; sacrifice; love; hope.

Story

Palm Sunday; Holy Week; Good Friday; Easter Sunday.

Symbol

Dove; candle; light; cross; crucified Christ; eggs; spring flowers; alpha/omega; Easter gardens; empty cross.

Celebration

Exchanging eggs; lighting Paschal candle; Easter processions; stations of the cross; Easter pilgrimage.

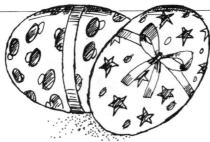

There is a danger in schools that the same festivals (particularly Christian ones) might be explored year after year by the pupils, with the same material introduced again and again. It is important, therefore, that as pupils progress through the school they gain a broader and deeper understanding of each festival. Teachers should plan carefully in order to maximize the pupils' opportunities for understanding.

Consider, for example, the festival of Christmas. Here is a festival which occupies a great deal of the timetable in primary schools during the autumn term and needs to be planned thoroughly throughout the school. Try this strategy.

1. First list key words/phrases describing what you consider the inner meaning of Christmas to be. Look at aspects of Christmas according to the circle model and list under the three headings suitable material which would lead children to encounter the inner meaning.

2. Now select for each year group in your school areas which you consider suitable for their ages and aptitudes, but ensure that each dimension of the model is represented at some stage during their time in school. Remember that pupils should build on previous learning and develop their understanding of Christmas through continuity and progression.

3. Devise some activities and events for each year group or class through which they will encounter the areas you suggest.

By the end of the exercise you should have some well-laid plans which will provide pupils with continuity and a developing understanding of Christmas throughout their primary education. Your plans may look something like this:

Christmas

Inner Meaning
Goodwill; love; celebration of a birthday; fulfilment of prophecy; God with us; peace; giving and receiving; God made man; sacrifice; . . .

Story
Stories of Jesus' birth; Papa Panov; Baboushka; St Lucia; . . .

Symbol
Star; light; candles; Christmas tree; crib scene; gold, frankincense and myrrh; angels; holly; . . .

Celebration
Carol singing; nativity plays; decorations; giving and receiving gifts; St Nicholas; . . .

KEY STAGE 1

Theme: 'Babies'

- General exploration of preparation for babies (i.e. decorate nursery, buy clothes, hang mobiles, etc.).
- How do we celebrate the birth of a baby? (Send cards, gifts and flowers, go to visit the baby, take photographs, etc.)
- Lead from this to Mary and Joseph expecting a baby so special that Christians remember his birth every year even though it happened long, long ago, and so special that people came to visit him, shepherds and wise men from a far-away country.
- Ask pupils to listen out for ways in which the following stories are different/similar to their experiences of the arrival of a new baby.
- Tell the story from Luke (2:1–20) about shepherds being told by angels to visit a special baby.
- Tell the story from Matthew (1:18–2:12) about how some astrologers followed a star, found a baby and gave him presents.
- Discuss with pupils which parts of the stories illustrate that Jesus was no ordinary baby, but that he was special (e.g. star, strange visitors with expensive gifts, angels, poor visitors).

It is important that pupils should not be taught something which has to be unlearned later on, so it is recommended that the birth of Jesus is told according to the gospel narratives, as separate stories of the same event. (There is no mention of a donkey, a stable or *three* kings in the gospel narratives.) Starting with the information from the texts, simply told, will provide pupils with a firm foundation on which to build their later understanding of the nature of story, the layers of meaning embodied within and how story is subject to interpretation. More important, pupils will begin to understand the significance of these stories to Christians throughout history and today.

KEY STAGE 2

The children might think about their own experiences and progress beyond them; the emphasis here might be on journeys or gifts.

Theme: 'Journeys'

- Discuss reasons for making journeys, preparation for journeys, excitement, anxieties, journeys the children have made, famous journeys in the news, etc.
- Lead on to the journey Mary and Joseph had to make and why. The reason might be related to what would happen if the Government ordered all members of the class to visit the towns where their fathers or mothers were born. The importance of David's City might be explored and the already acquired knowledge about the visitors could be built in.

Theme: 'Gifts'

- Ask pupils to consider their 'gifts' or 'talents' and produce pictures of themselves demonstrating these.
- Discuss 'How does my gift help others?'
- Tell the story of Papa Panov (by Leo Tolstoy) and discuss his gifts and talents.
- Consider what makes different people happy (family and friends) and list suitable 'free' gifts for them (e.g. help Dad with washing up, give Gran a hug, let my brother play with my toys).
- Consider other gift-bringers and what their gifts entailed (e.g. St Lucia, St Nicholas).

KEY STAGE 3

Theme: 'Symbols at Christmas'

- In groups, brainstorm Christmas for symbols (e.g. Christmas trees, star, crib, magi, dove).
- Direct each group to select a symbol and investigate and discuss its meaning and the story it tells.
- Direct pupils to prepare a presentation to the class through drama, artwork or narration explaining their findings.
- Explore with pupils the symbolism of the gifts of the magi (Matthew 1 and 2): gold, a precious metal fit for a king; frankincense, an incense used in worship – Jesus is worthy of worship; myrrh, an embalming ointment for the dead – prophecy of Jesus' death.
- Provide a selection of Christmas cards, both secular and religious.
- Direct pupils to classify them into groups: religious or secular.
- Direct them to classify them according to symbols.
- Direct pupils to classify religious cards according to the birth narrative of Matthew or Luke (with reference to the texts).

These ideas serve only as starting-points and there are glaring omissions which teachers may want to include. The Annunciation (Luke 1:26–33), for example, is a beautiful but difficult-to-grasp passage which could be introduced to older pupils. Our class can begin to appreciate the message which it contains, that the child to be born was special so his coming was heralded in a special way. 'Angel', *angellos* in Greek, means 'messenger' and the emphasis should not be upon wings and haloes but upon the pronouncement in Luke 1:30–32. This links up with King David and Bethlehem, and with choosing a name, which have already been mentioned. Mary's response in the form of the *Magnificat* should be read.

By Key Stage 3 pupils should be familiar with the two distinct accounts of the birth of Jesus and realize that the Gospel of Luke expresses the universality of God's kingdom. Jesus is portrayed as born into poverty and is visited by shepherds – who were among those Jews least able to keep the Torah fully. Luke's message is that the Messiah came for everyone, even the outcasts, yet his true nature is revealed by the angels who visit the shepherds. They herald a new age and reveal Jesus as the promised saviour.

The Gospel of Matthew, however, portrays a Jesus descended from King David, and Jesus' ancestors are listed (Matthew 1:2–16). No suggestion is made of a lowly birth in this gospel, but instead magi, important religious leaders, travel from the East to visit Jesus, bringing him extravagant gifts. The emphasis here is on the fulfilment of Jewish hopes: the hope of a king like David who would rule the nation in freedom and peace; the hope of a new prophet like Moses who would announce the coming of a new age.

The perceptive will have noticed that no reference has been made to Mary's unmarried state and the virginal conception. We would leave these to the secondary school, where pupils should be able to consider the theological issues rather than concentrate on the facts.

Of course we must not pretend that things actually progress as smoothly and logically as this framework may suggest! There will be ten-year-olds who know almost nothing of the Christmas story except for the *three* kings, the shepherds and the stable (we've met them), and there will be others who know everything including Mary's unmarried state. In these circumstances teachers must rely on their professional good sense. What we are trying to do is to help teachers create a better approach to RE, in this case studying Christmas.

Before we leave this aspect of RE and school in general, which is often the bane of the teacher's life, here are some ways to ring the changes besides the topics we have referred to:

- Look at Christmas in another European country (most Asians and Africans have adopted the practices of the nations which colonized them, including snow scenes on Christmas cards).
- Do a project on Christmas past (medieval or Victorian).
- Base a topic on Christmas customs.
- Faced with bored top-junior/middle-school children who know it all, set them a quiz using old cards, pictures and Bible passages, displayed on the walls (e.g. 'How many kings were there?', 'Which gospels tell the story of Jesus' birth?', 'Why do we have robins on cards?', 'Name Royal David's City.'). After a few days get them to share their findings and show how much they actually did know.

But whatever the approach we must not lose sight of the RE aim, which is to understand what the birth of Jesus means to Christians. Until children reach the secondary school we may only be able to hint at this, however the various aspects of the story and the ways it is celebrated are ultimately peripheral to the significance that it has for the believer.

Having explored the festival of Christmas in depth, you may like to develop schemes of work for other festivals.

CHAPTER
15
VISITS
AND VISITORS

Teachers can provide for pupils an exciting RE menu using role-play, simulation, slides, videos, music, art and craft activities, cookery and so on, but probably the event which would provide the most impact would be a visit to a place of interest or a visitor to the school. Visits and visitors can bring theory to life for pupils, and are well worth the effort and time spent in preparation. But care in organization is essential or a potentially valuable occasion can go sadly awry.

Visitors

When thinking of suitable visitors who can contribute to the religious education of pupils, leaders of faith communities naturally come to mind, but think again – the possibilities are much broader. What is of paramount importance, of course, is the visitors' ability to communicate with young children, so they should be either known personally to the teacher or highly recommended by a colleague or another school.

Leaders of faith communities, such as the rabbi, the imam or the vicar, can be helpful and are often willing and able to explore areas of religion with young children, but the assumption must not be made that because they are used to addressing congregations and groups, then they will be good at speaking to youngsters. Some may think that they are but the pupils think otherwise!

These people may speak with passion and authority about their faith, which can be illuminating for older pupils, but teachers will be aware that younger pupils may feel intimidated, confused or disturbed by such exhortations. Choose visitors with caution.

With the thematic approach in mind, you might like to consider, perhaps with colleagues, a variety of people who could contribute something worthwhile to the RE dimension of 'Food', 'The Senses' or 'Water'. The examples given for 'Books' may help.

Theme: 'Books'

Possible visitors are:

- the local librarian to talk about books which appear to be current favourites with children;

- a local grandmother/father who may have a very old, precious book they are willing to show the class and to talk about;
- a member of a faith community (a vicar, imam, or Muslim parent) who could bring his or her holy book and talk to the pupils about it.

Both the visitor and the pupils need to feel that the occasion is relaxed and worthwhile, so the following procedures may provide a helpful check-list.

1. Brief the visitor fully on the purpose of the visit, where the event fits into the overall scheme, the time allocated, what you hope to achieve, what the pupils have already explored on the subject, their ages and number, the location of the meeting (in the classroom, hall or library) and the form of presentation required (slides, music, discussion or interview). Tell him/her clearly and precisely your requirements and put this in writing in the form of a back-up letter.

2. Prepare the pupils so that the visit is understood in context, and so that they can consider suitable questions to ask should the opportunity arise.

3. Make arrangements for the visitor's transport and expenses and offer hospitality to demonstrate your welcome.

4. Arrange the classroom or hall *before* the visitor arrives and have the required equipment set up. Displays on the subject to be addressed will enhance the visit and a well-prepared room will aid the flow of proceedings and provide a relaxed atmosphere.

Visits

Places of worship seem the most obvious choice when planning RE visits for pupils, but look out also for exhibitions and events, sometimes local or sometimes in the major cities, in museums, art galleries or exhibition centres. There may be an exhibition of the Bishop's vestments in a nearby town hall which could contribute to a topic on clothes, or perhaps an Indian group are dancing aspects of the Ramayana at the local arts centre when your class is exploring Diwali, or you might visit the Victoria and Albert Museum to see Buddha rupa (images of the Buddha) as a contribution to a theme on signs and symbols.

Clearly, whenever teachers plan a visit careful preparations should be made. We need not expound on obvious necessities like locating the loos, booking the coach and checking facilities for eating packed lunches. Perhaps, however, there are less obvious preparations which need to be made before an RE visit.

You might like to write down a check-list which would help a probationary teacher planning an RE trip, then compare notes with a colleague.

You may have included a preparatory visit to the suggested location. It is very important that teachers are familiar with the potential of a place to visit, that they discover what the guides or curators have to offer and that the visit is planned accordingly. Parents are required to pay for visits and will expect that not only are the pupils enthusiastic, but the trip is well worth the financial investment on educational grounds. A trip needs to be fun, stimulating and contribute to the pupils' knowledge and understanding.

During the preparatory visit, teachers will need to note items of specific interest so that worksheets, activity packs or trails can be prepared for pupils, if appropriate. Some museums produce their own worksheets, but they do not always meet the needs of individual classes, and places of worship rarely provide such documents (with the exception of some cathedrals). They may, however, provide information sheets, slide packs and postcards which would be useful for preparatory or follow-up work in the classroom.

In some cases, a visit can be geared to suit the teacher's particular plans. If this is the case, then the representative from the building (a gurdwara, church or synagogue, for example) needs to be fully aware of the purpose of the visit and what s/he is required to do. If pupils are exploring religious signs and symbols, a visit to the local church would be wasted if the vicar talked about his work in the parish!

If planning a visit to a place of worship, teachers should ask a representative about any rules of dress or codes of conduct. Head coverings, removal of shoes, boys and girls sitting separately may be some of the requirements about which the pupils will need to be prepared, and naturally, they should know that speaking and moving quietly and respectfully is essential when entering a place of worship.

Of course, parents will be informed of the planned visit, but a clear explanation about its purpose and its contribution to the overall scheme of work will clarify for parents the value of an educational visit and avoid any potential misunderstandings. It might be prudent to invite them along!

CHAPTER
16

SCHOOL WORSHIP

Should a book on religious education include a section on school worship?

We thought about this question for some time. There were a number of reasons why we were inclined to leave out worship. One was that it is a separate area of the curriculum in its own right. We didn't want to give the impression that it is a job for the person who is responsible for co-ordinating RE in the school. The Act (40:6:3) places the responsibility in maintained schools firmly on the shoulders of the headteacher after consultation with the governing body. (In voluntary-aided schools the roles are reversed; the governing body is responsible after consultation with the headteacher.)

Secondly, we would argue that this book is about religious education and that, therefore, school worship has no more and no less place in it than it would have in a book on teaching science or history. After all the Education Reform Act distinguishes between school worship and religious education, making it clear that they are not synonymous and that schools which think that they have met the legal requirement on religious education by holding an act of worship are breaking the law. However, we eventually decided to include the chapter because, to be realistic, the association of worship with classroom RE, which dates back to the 1944 Education Act, still persists in many schools. Also, by refusing to be involved, the RE co-ordinator is depriving the school of his/her expertise and may be left to put together the shattered spirit of the school in the staffroom and classroom after some unfortunate experience in the hall!

From the general tone of this book you will have realized that we view RE like any other curriculum area. No special pleading that ours is a Christian country or that Christian bodies were the first providers of education, therefore religion has a right to be included in what children study in school. Our case rests purely on the argument that beliefs and values are as important as the study of the past or of geography or the arts or the sciences and politics in the education of anyone who is to live a full life. What they make of their knowledge is up to them. They may never listen to another piece of music or visit a museum but they have been made aware of how music and history are to be appreciated and understood and of the way in which they impinge on the lives of human beings and societies. So it is with beliefs and values. Children should know, be informed, be aware of the importance of beliefs and values and equipped to develop their own world view, but the teacher in a maintained school has no right to take things further. The privilege of nurturing children in a particular faith belongs to the home and to the believing community, the church or the mosque, it is not a responsibility that should be required of teachers. You will not be surprised that we, together with many other specialists in religious education, do not approve of school worship in the form we suspect the Government envisaged. We are very much in favour of school assemblies and suggest below ways in which the Act can be interpreted positively.

First you might like to consider the arguments for and against school worship and write them down before reading further.

Your list might include such things as:

- Children enjoy singing hymns.
- The things we do aren't really religious, none of our teachers find them threatening.
- Children need to learn the Lord's Prayer.
- They don't get any religion at home so if we don't give them some they won't receive any at all.
- Children need to experience religion, not just learn about it. Aren't we giving way to secularism if we abolish worship?
- I can't be hypocritical: I don't go to church and I shouldn't be asked to encourage children to pray, and believe in God.

To these we would reply:

- Yes, children do like singing hymns. Most of them like singing anything. They would sing the Internationale with gusto! Hymns affirm belief and offer praise. We shouldn't compare them with other songs and, consequently, implicitly encourage children to think that faith is natural and easy.
- If what we do isn't really religious aren't we deceiving children about the true nature of belief and worship and the commitment which is involved? Are they really experiencing religion? The ignorance in which their parents keep them might be better than this.
- Children can, and should learn the Lord's Prayer – and the Shema and other passages from a variety of faiths at the appropriate time as part of their religious education – but they should learn it as the prayer which Jesus taught his disciples to say, not as something to be uttered regardless of discipleship. Honesty seems to be a rare commodity in our society, we should be encouraging teachers and children to be honest.
- The argument of a religious sell-out is perhaps the most difficult to deal with. Certainly it is well used by MPs and some bishops in Parliament. However, we are of the opinion that it is better to face the reality that school worship provokes hostile and negative attitudes among teachers and secondary pupils rather than to hold on to what is regarded as a privilege. In doing so we are not bowing to their pressures but to what lies behind them, namely respect for the individual and respect for religion. The requirement for a compulsory act of worship seems to neglect both of these.
- Worship is affirmative, education in Britain is critical and questioning. Though some people can combine a questioning attitude to life with a religious belief it seems inadvisable to put children in our schools into that situation. The context of a child in a believing home or voluntarily attending Sunday school is altogether different, though the clash between traditional faith and the challenge of a secular society which has no place for the assumptions of faith is to be found in many of the most devout homes! School worship

stands out as an educational sore thumb and an embarrassment to those who take seriously the importance of personal faith.

- There is no answer to the hypocrisy argument. Teachers and children who are asked to affirm what they do not believe are being required to be hypocritical!

All this is not very helpful to the headteacher who faces a visit by an inspector next Monday. What can we do on Monday to meet the legal requirement of the 1988 Act?

First we must ensure that every child, at some time during the day, takes part in an 'act of worship', unless a formal request has been received from a parent.

Secondly, what we provide, taking the term as a whole, must be worship wholly or mainly of a broadly Christian nature. However, it must not be distinctive of any particular denomination and must take into account the family backgrounds of the children as well as their ages and aptitudes. This means that we are engaged in an educational exercise in worshipping just as much as when we teach mathematics or any other subject. 'Age and aptitude' requires us to operate at the level of the pupils taking into account what they can understand, and if we know that their 'family background' is not at all religious that is a further factor to be considered. The affirmative worship which nourishes mature Christians and that which the Act envisages are two very different activities.

Consequently, at springtime a group of young primary children might be invited to think about the beauty and colours which surround them. They could talk about some of the seasonal things they like. The eggs they might be receiving at Easter could be related to the symbolism of new life. A spring song could be sung. 'Age and aptitude' would exclude explicit reference to ideas of creation or the Easter story.

The same topic with ten-year-olds could examine the way in which spring has prompted some men and women, like the psalmist in Psalm 19, for example, to think about the world and see the hand of God in it. During the week they might listen to readings which express a variety of responses to spring, not all of them religious. A prayer might be read and the children encouraged to listen to it and reflect on it.

We would defend this 'thought for the day' approach as one which respects the child, the teacher, and the religion. The silent response may be more profound than joining together to say a prayer or sing a hymn. A similar example in the infant school might start as follows:

'It is springtime with green leaves breaking out on the trees and late hyacinths and tulips in flower in the gardens.'

Examples of these can be brought into the hall so that attention is drawn to them and children can be invited to reflect upon the new growth and varieties of green where, a few weeks ago, everything seemed dead. New times in their lives might be discussed or the focus kept on the natural world. Songs might be sung or one class might perform a flower dance. A poem could be read. We feel it would be enough to end with:

'Look around you. See how many shades of green/new things you can see today.'

Some teachers might feel that they could or should go further. They might add:

'Some people look at all these wonderful things and say, "It couldn't just happen." They say that there must be a wonderful being whom they call God who made it all. Let's listen to a poem/prayer by someone who wants to thank God for the beauty of the world.'

(Of course somehow the word 'God' must have already been invested with meaning. If it hasn't been, or cannot be it would be inadvisable simply to introduce the word through this or any other assembly, though we suspect that teachers do so in the hope that somehow the concept will take care of itself.)

In a top-junior/middle-school assembly (Key Stage 3), if the Easter story has been covered in class, it would be possible to link new life in the natural world with the death and resurrection of Jesus, not that it is a form of proof, but because St Paul (1 Corinthians 15) used natural imagery in this way and so have many Christian poets.

> 'So,' the teacher could go on, 'when Christians go to church on Easter Day they might see an Easter garden [describe, make one] and find the church decorated with flowers because spring reminds Christians of the resurrection of Jesus.'

A poem or prayer focused on Easter could be read and the children invited to think about it.

An act of worship on friendship at Key Stage 1 would concentrate on the experiences of the children: what they do with their friends, why they like a friend to go with them when they have to run an errand for teacher or Mum. They could be told about Jesus journeying around Palestine (or Israel?) with his friends. On other days they could hear about David and his friend Jonathan, Guru Nanak and his companion Mardana, and Muhammad and his companions, depending on circumstances.

At Key Stage 2 it would be possible to consider the reliability of Jesus' friends, especially through the story of Peter and if one of the classes had been doing work on this episode in the life of Jesus. (Assemblies are excellent opportunities for children to share with the rest of the school what they have been doing in class but care must be taken to avoid a spirit of inter-class or inter-teacher competition.)

The Act requires the majority of acts of worship in a term to be 'wholly or mainly of a broadly Christian character' and DES circular 3/89, which is not a legal document but something to be taken very seriously, states:

> in the secretary of state's view, an act of worship which is 'broadly Christian' need not contain only Christian material, provided that, taken as a whole, it reflects the traditions of Christian belief. (para 34)

This would allow Muslim, Sikh or Humanist insights on these themes of spring, new life, the natural world, or friendship, and many others, to be included.

With care and tact the good practices of the past decade or more can be retained and developed. There is no need to go to the Standing Advisory Council on Religious Education to obtain a determination allowing worship to be multifaith, though faith communities were so upset by the 1988 Act that it might be a wise and sensible thing to do. The inclusion of 'Christian' in the Act should certainly not be seen as an opportunity to impose that kind of worship which is unsuitable when the age, aptitude, and family background of our primary-school children are considered.

Assemblies, non-worshipping gatherings of children, can have immense value. They can be opportunities for exploration and celebration, for welding together the school as a unity but for expressing the diversity which must exist within any such community as well. They can be times when Eid or Pesach (Passover), and Christmas can be shared but in an open way not limited by the constraint to pray or praise. Such assemblies as we have in mind are to be found in *Exploring Primary Assemblies*, edited by Warwick Griffin (Macmillan, 1984). They cannot be dismissed as trivial or of little worth and are educationally sound. They demonstrate how worthwhile assemblies can be. We would argue that those assemblies can be used still even in our post-ERA schools. The way ahead must be that indicated in books like that of Warwick Griffin and in an easing of the requirement to assemble daily.

In 1987 the Churches recognized the difficulties caused by the clause demanding a daily act of worship and were willing to see it relaxed. It was Parliament that insisted that there should be no change, fearing that any alteration would be interpreted as a dilution of the Christian faith of the country. We hope that the clauses on worship which were eventually enacted, and which we consider to be unwise and potentially harmful, will not be used by Muslims and others as a reason for withdrawal and for demanding their own voluntary-aided schools, or by Christians as a means of promoting their beliefs. The goodwill of teachers, the fundamental unity of society, and the freedom of the individual, especially the very young, should not be threatened in this way.

For further information, see *Worship in Education,* published by the Council of Churches for Britain and Ireland (address on p. 99), price £2.95.

CHAPTER
17

SUMMING UP AND LOOKING AHEAD

Religious education has come a long way since 1944. Nurture and the telling of Bible stories have given way to the understanding of religion, the teaching of Christianity in all of its many aspects, including the Bible, together with the serious examination of other religions. Some teachers have not come this far, of course. We have already drawn attention to the non-existence of religious education in some primary schools. In others there is little evidence of change but in many there is enthusiasm and good religious education being provided. Many readers of this book might want to stop and catch their breath before going any further along the path of curriculum development. They have our sympathy. In our more jaundiced moments we might wonder at the fact that they have actually found time to read even this short book, such are the demands of the post-1988 curriculum! We are compelled, however, by the very logic of our approach to point to a number of issues which still demand attention as we look towards the future.

Openness　How open can religious education be while the requirement to worship is still placed upon schools? Some teachers believe that neither religious education nor religion, especially Christianity, benefits from this constraint. Perhaps it is for the religions to give a lead here and seriously consider what kind of expression of belief, if any, is appropriate in the schools of the nineties and beyond. Certainly much more educational as opposed to political attention needs to be given to the separate curriculum area of school worship than it has so far received.

Key Stage 1　We look towards a religious education which will develop at Key Stage 1, a matter that is only beginning to be addressed. Immediately upon their arrival in school, some children from homes in which religion does not exist find themselves presented with 'God language' in a manner which is often confusing and can be harmful. Understanding 'God language' is a vital part of RE but this has to be done in an open setting. Giving due place and respect to naturalistic or non-religious interpretations of existence is important. This does not mean selling out to science as popularly understood. Most people, true scientists included, actually believe that there is more to life than materialism. Compassion, the creation of beauty, the appreciation of the natural world, are human characteristics. So often bad religious education seems to deny this and 'God answers' are provided exclusively, even when they are inappropriate. This perpetuates a dichotomy between science and religion which may no longer really exist. Much more attention to Key Stage 1, especially, is needed. Its importance in providing the foundation of all education cannot be stressed too much.

The concept of God   Despite the points made in the previous paragraph, there is still the need to invest the concept of God with meaning progressively. Many grown ups have a view of God which has not developed beyond that which they held in childhood. Some responsibility for this must lie with us as teachers. Whilst not wishing to force belief upon children, we are concerned that their religious understanding should develop throughout their years in school. In multifaith religious education we are, of course, talking of concepts of God, in the plural.

Religious education, the exploration of beliefs and values, call it what we will, is probably the most difficult, exciting and rewarding curriculum area to teach in the schools of a liberal democracy where we wish to enable children to become adults who can think for themselves and formulate their own ideas and views. The 1988 Education Reform Act charges teachers with preparing 'pupils for the opportunities, responsibilities and experiences of adult life'.

Success in meeting the requirement to teach religious education depends on:

- more time being given to religious education in B.Ed. curriculum courses;
- more time being given to religious education in PGCE curriculum courses;
- more INSET provision by LEAs;
- more support by LEAs in the form of advisers/inspectors and advisory teachers;
- a general recognition by governments and society that a nation's well-being is more than a matter of economics and that a school curriculum which emphasizes economic considerations to the neglect of those things that make us human, such as the creative arts, literature, the study of the past, as well as the exploration of beliefs and values, is actually dehumanizing.

Of one thing we are certain, there can be no turning back to the kind of education which children were given in most schools before 1945. The complexities of society, not only because it is multireligious, the nature of the world and the place of Britain in it convince us of the need for children to be educated to live full lives as citizens of the next generation. Religious education has a positive role to play in broadening horizons, stimulating thought and encouraging flexibility. Religions may be liberating or stifling in their influence on individuals and societies, so may educational processes. We are for approaches to both which are life enhancing.

RESOURCES

Teachers who are not specialists in religious studies are likely to want to know where they can obtain information about the six major religions found in Britain today. We would point them to a number of books written for GCSE pupils hoping that they will not be offended but realize that it is these not the academic tomes which often have sections on how and why people worship, celebrate festivals, and engage in the other activities which tend to be the main content of primary RE.

On specific religions we direct teachers to the *World Religions* series, published by Stanley Thornes. *Hinduism, Christianity* and *Sikhism* are already available. *Buddhism* and *Islam* are in preparation at the time of writing (May 1991). Two books which each cover all six religions are *Religions*, by Alan Brown, John Rankin and Angela Wood (Longman), and *Six Religions in the Twentieth Century*, by Owen Cole and Peggy Morgan (Stanley Thornes). This last book concentrates on the themes of messengers, pilgrimage, scriptures, worship and festivals. *Five World Faiths*, edited by Owen Cole (Cassell), omits Buddhism.

A major resource manual and reference book is *Teaching World Religions*, edited by Clive Erricker (Heinemann, 1993). Alan Brown has edited *Festivals in World Religions* (Longman), which provides information about most of the festivals celebrated worldwide. Further information about festivals can be found in the excellent RMEP series *Living Festivals*, which has currently 23 titles. Photocopyable teacher's books accompany the series.

Another useful compendium is the Berkshire Handbook, *Religious Heritage and Personal Quest; Principles into Practice*, which deserves to be known far beyond the boundaries of the royal county. This contains bibliographies relating to particular themes as does *Religious Education Topics for the Primary School*, by John Rankin, Alan Brown and Mary Hayward (Longman). The series *Stories from the Religions of the World* (Simon & Schuster, also obtainable from RMEP) is a valuable source of material from the Christian, Hindu, Jewish, Muslim, and Sikh traditions.

Updating information is difficult. So many books keep appearing, not always written by authors who are comfortable in the area of religious studies. We advise every school, therefore, to subscribe to the Christian Education Movement's termly mailing entitled *Exploring a Theme* and more recently *Teaching Religion*. Titles have included *Food, Exploring Christianity, Leaders*, and *Symbols*. Further details can be obtained from CEM (address below). Equally essential is the annual *Journal* of the Shap Working Party on World Religions in Education. This includes an annual *Calendar* of religious festivals and may be purchased from Alan Brown, c/o The National Society's RE Centre (address below).

Shap also offers a **free information service** provided by:

> Vida Barnett
> 81 St Mary's Road
> Huyton
> Merseyside L36 5SR

Those teachers who wish to use it should provide a self-addressed envelope with enough stamps to cover postage and be as precise as possible in their requests. It has been known for Vida to receive a letter with no SAE saying: 'I'm doing a topic on Hinduism. Can you help me?' Vida did but details of the age range and something clearer like 'Hindu worship' or 'the symbolism of water in Hinduism' would have enabled a more satisfactory reply to be given!

We are not giving an exhaustive list of books for the classroom as this would be duplicating information contained in the books already mentioned but we do recommend that the school library should possess all the books in the *Religions of the World* series (Simon & Schuster, also available from RMEP). *The Christian World*, by Alan Brown, is probably the best book on that religion available for top junior/middle school and a model of the kind of approach in Christian textbooks that we would encourage. It and the companion volumes will enable pupils to put together into a coherent whole the areas which they have explored thematically.

Teachers wishing to think more about the Education Reform Act can do no better than to read *The Act Unpacked*, by John Hull (CEM). It is very brief but extremely perceptive. *Worship in Education*, produced by the British Council of Churches (now the Council of Churches for Britain and Ireland – address below), was written to help teachers, school governors and SACREs think their way through this difficult curriculum area.

A book which is intended to assist teachers in understanding the cultural background of children whose parental background is Caribbean, Asian or Jewish and in providing them with an appropriate religious education is *Religion in the Multifaith School*, edited by Owen Cole (Stanley Thornes). A recent Church of England publication looking at religious education in Anglican primary schools is *Holy Ground, World Faiths in Primary Schools*, written by R. O. Hughes, John Sargant and David Webb for the Diocese of Salisbury. A new resource for teaching about Christianity is *Teaching Christianity*, by W. Owen Cole and Ruth Mantin (Heinemann Educational, 1994).

From this bibliographical survey the RE co-ordinator and headteacher should be able to provide the kind of information which is essential if enthusiasm and goodwill are to be turned into good practice.

Addresses for organizations mentioned above:

Christian Education Movement
Royal Buildings
Victoria Street
Derby DE1 1GW

The National Society's RE Centre
23 Kensington Square
London W8 5HN

Council of Churches for Britain and Ireland
35–41 Lower Marsh
London SE1 7RL

Some other addresses which teachers are likely to find most useful are:

AMANA
11 Weltje Road
London W6 9TG
Telephone 081-748-2424

Dedicated to fostering a greater understanding of Islam in Britain, this is an important source for materials and advice on all aspects of Islam, especially in education. Among its members are practising teachers, some of whom serve on SACREs.

Articles of Faith
Christine and Leslie Howard
Bury Business Centre
Kay Street
Bury BL9 6BU
Telephone 061-705-1878

The best source for artefacts for all the main religions except Judaism. A catalogue is available.

Buddhist Society
58 Ecclestone Square
London SWIV 1PH

Provides lists for teachers and help in putting them in touch with local Buddhist organizations.

ISKCON Educational Services
Bhakti Vedanta Manor
Letchmore
Hertfordshire WD2 8EP
Telephone 0923-859578

Can help with speakers on Hinduism and in finding temples to visit. They also provide excellent literature.

Jewish Education Bureau
8 Westcombe Avenue
Leeds LS8 2BS

Rabbi Douglas Charing, its director, is a well-respected figure in the RE world. This is the best source for Jewish artefacts, books and AVA, as well as advice. A catalogue is available.

British Sikh Educational Council
10 Featherstone Road
Southall
Middlesex UB1 5AA

Run by Sikh educationalists who can offer advice on teaching about their religion.

Please send an SAE when contacting any of the above addresses.

An excellent source for posters is Pictorial Charts Educational Trust (distributors: CEM, address above).

Teaching World Religions, already mentioned, contains a more detailed list.

APPENDIX

The following letter is important for clarifying and amplifying the purpose and content of religious education under the 1988 Act. For this reason we reproduce it in full.

THE DEPARTMENT OF EDUCATION & SCIENCE

To: All Chief Education Officers
        in England

18 March 1991

Dear Colleague,

As you are no doubt aware, the Secretary of State has been considering certain complaints about agreed syllabuses for religious education in schools. The issue is whether the syllabuses comply with Section 8(3) of the Education Reform Act 1988 which provides that all agreed syllabuses adopted after 29 September 1988 must:

"reflect the fact that the religious traditions in Great Britain are in the main Christian whilst taking account of the teaching and practices of the other principal religions represented in Great Britain."

The Secretary of State is not, of course, able to provide a definitive interpretation of the law; this is a matter for the courts. In the course of considering these complaints he has, however, taken advice as to the view a court would be likely to take about the nature of an agreed syllabus which it would deem to comply with the statutory provisions. Given the responsibility of local education authorities for drawing up agreed syllabuses, he believes it would be helpful to make this information available more widely, as follows.

It seems likely that the Court, if asked to rule on the point, would find that a syllabus which is to meet the statutory requirements must give sufficient particulars for it to be clear that the teaching carried out in pursuance of that syllabus would be consistent with the requirements of the provision.

Given the wording of Section 8(3), the Secretary of State is advised that an agreed syllabus which meets its requirements, and thus the content of religious education given in accordance with the syllabus, must devote a reasonable amount of attention to teaching based on Christian traditions. The fact that the religious traditions in Great Britain are in the main Christian would in most cases be properly reflected by devoting most attention to Christian traditions; however an agreed syllabus which conforms with Section 8(3) cannot confine itself exclusively to religious education based on Christian traditions, or exclude from its teaching any of the principal religions represented in Great Britain. The precise balance of the content would need to be determined locally in the light of local factors, such as the composition of the local community.

Having regard to the statutory provisions an agreed syllabus should also:

- not be denominational;
- not be designed to convert pupils, or to urge a particular religion or religious belief on pupils;
- be based on Christianity and other major religions and on their religious traditions, practices and teaching, and indicate which of such matters should appropriately be taught at various ages and times;
- not be confined to information about religions and religious traditions, practices and teaching, but extend to wider areas of morality including the difference between right and wrong, and the effect that religious beliefs and practices have on people's daily lives;
- have regard to the national as well as the local position, though decisions about content are to be made at local level through the Conference convened to draw up the syllabus: such decisions should have regard to the local school population and the need to satisfy the wishes of local parents so as to avoid great numbers of them exercising their right of withdrawal.

It follows that, whether a new agreed syllabus complies with the law should not be tested against such shorthand phrases as "mainly Christian" or "multifaith". Such shorthand phrases do not encapsulate all the requirements of the Section.

In the light of the above, the Secretary of State is not satisfied that an agreed syllabus could fully meet the requirements of Section 8(3) unless it gives sufficient guidance to the reader, and thus the teacher, as to what Christian traditions, learning, teaching and festivals are going to be taught and what elements are going to be taught in respect of the other principal religions represented in Great Britain.

I am copying this letter to all CEOs in England and to the National Curriculum Council.

Yours sincerely,

A E D CHAMIER
Schools 3 Branch